A PLACE IN HISTORY

Fifty more East Anglian moments in time

PETER SARGENT

Also by **Peter Sargent**

A Moment in Time (2017)

A PLACE IN HISTORY

Fifty more East Anglian moments in time

If stones could talk: Statue at Crowland Abbey in the Lincolnshire fens.

A Place in History

Fifty stories that bring East Anglian history to life

First published in Great Britain in paperback, September 2018
by Paul Dickson, 8 Bridge Court, Fishergate, Norwich NR3 1UE
Tel: 01603 666011
paul-dickson@btconnect.com

ISBN Paperback 978-0-9956187-6-3
A CIP catalogue record of this book is available from the British Library.

Cover design by Andy Elsom
Photographs by the author and courtesy Rusty Aldwinckle, The Sealed Knot.
Printed in Norwich by InterPrint

To my Mother, who set the ball rolling with all those library books.

Places in history

Guide to the locations featured. The numbers on the map relate to chapter numbers. **See Pages 11 and 12.**

10 Birth of Lynn

36 Fanny Burney

King's Lynn

Crowland

8 Tom Hickathrift

20 Katharine of Aragon

24 Warboys witches

Wisbech

Peterborough

42 Thomas Clarkson

48 Octavia Hill

23 Kirby Hall

7 Birth of England

Huntingdon

12 Disinherited barons

Cambridge

Map not to scale

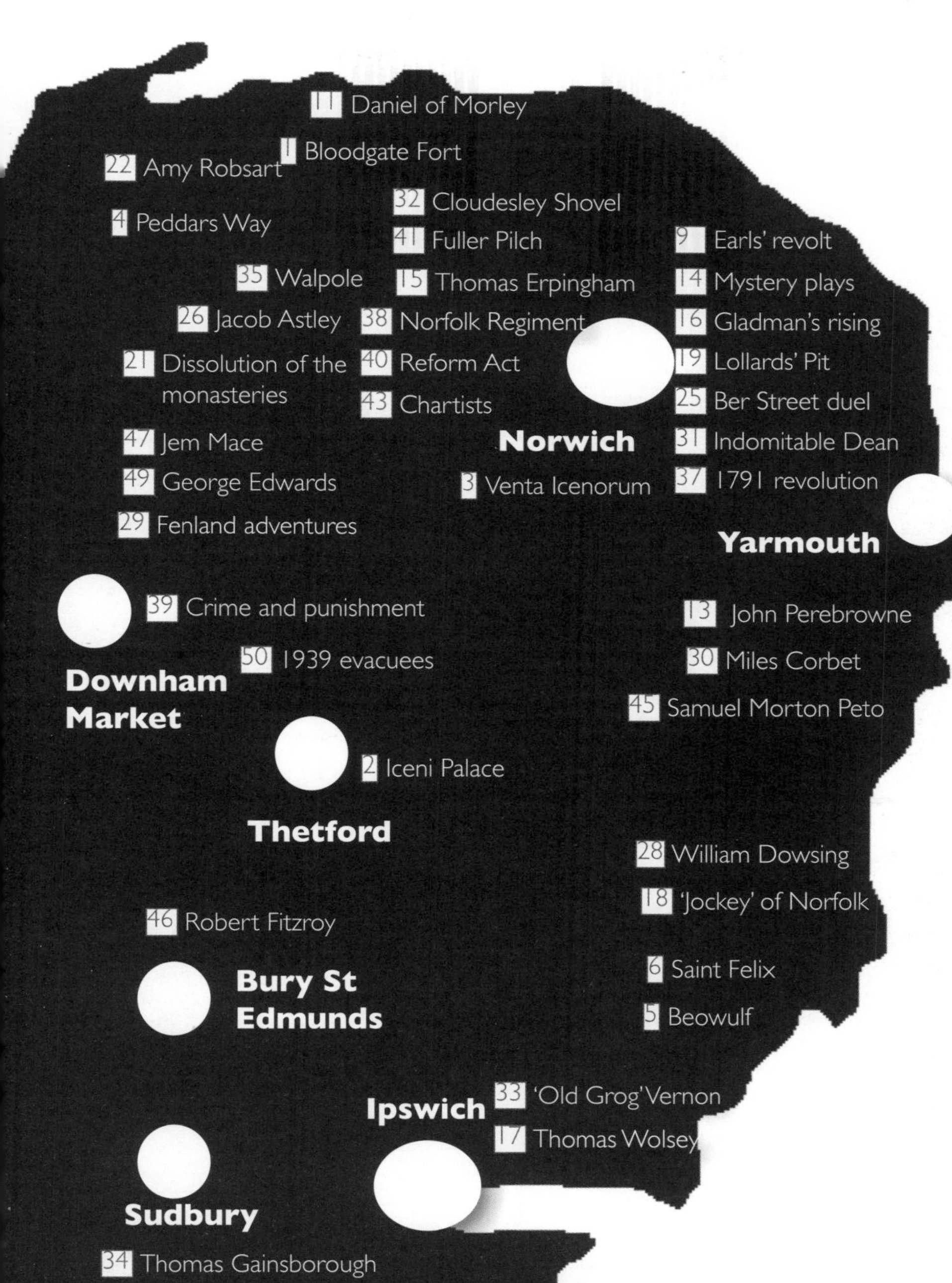
11 Daniel of Morley
1 Bloodgate Fort
22 Amy Robsart
32 Cloudesley Shovel
4 Peddars Way
41 Fuller Pilch
9 Earls' revolt
35 Walpole
15 Thomas Erpingham
14 Mystery plays
26 Jacob Astley
38 Norfolk Regiment
16 Gladman's rising
21 Dissolution of the monasteries
40 Reform Act
19 Lollards' Pit
43 Chartists
25 Ber Street duel
47 Jem Mace
Norwich
31 Indomitable Dean
49 George Edwards
3 Venta Icenorum
37 1791 revolution
29 Fenland adventures
Yarmouth
39 Crime and punishment
13 John Perebrowne
50 1939 evacuees
30 Miles Corbet
Downham Market
45 Samuel Morton Peto
2 Iceni Palace
Thetford
28 William Dowsing
18 'Jockey' of Norfolk
46 Robert Fitzroy
6 Saint Felix
Bury St Edmunds
5 Beowulf
33 'Old Grog' Vernon
Ipswich
17 Thomas Wolsey
Sudbury
34 Thomas Gainsborough

Introduction

This book is a sequel to my first publication A Moment in Time, which appeared in 2017. It follows a similar format to the original, in that there are 50 more stories bringing East Anglian history to life. Imagine a couple of history enthusiasts enjoying a discussion in their local pub, probably over a pint of foaming beer, and you will get the picture. This is history, with a slightly wry smile.

This time the focus is as much on places as it is on people and events. In these pages you will find tales of an Iron Age fort in north Norfolk, a Roman road seemingly leading to nowhere, the locations in East Anglia visited by determined Christian saints working to convert the Anglo-Saxons and the castles and churches built to impress the neighbours during the medieval period.

There are stately homes lovingly created by the aristocracy, the Norwich street where a bloody duel was fought and an iconic abbey town in the Lincolnshire fens besieged by Oliver Cromwell during the English Civil War.

The beautiful Suffolk landscape immortalised by Thomas Gainsborough is featured, along with historic Norwich hotel The Maids Head, where a group of idealistic revolutionaries sat down to dinner in 1791. In the fenland town of Wisbech we look at the spot where courageous anti-slavery campaigner Thomas Clarkson is immortalised. Back in Norwich we visit the site of the pub where 19th Century bare-knuckle champion boxer, world traveller and colourful character Jem Mace was once the landlord. We'll see where the railways came and transformed people's lives. Finally, we'll consider the enormous impact of evacuation of families from city to country at the start of the Second World War in 1939.

Once again there is a varied cast list; saints and sinners, scholars and soldiers, sportsmen and sailors, rogues and writers, revolutionaries and reactionaries. They all have their place in history, as you'll discover in these pages.

As in my first publication, some of these stories first saw life in the pages of the Eastern Daily Press newspaper, but others are freshly discovered and published here for the first time.

Among the many people to thank are the Heritage Guides of Crowland for their generous help in providing information on the Civil War siege there, Mr Peter Mansel James, of Norwich, for letting me know the tale of his distant forebear Robert Mansel and the Ber Street duel, Pete Kelley for his proof-reading skills, Andy Elsom for his work on the cover, and also the Sealed Knot and photographer Rusty Aldwinckle for permission to use their fine pictures. Not forgetting, of course, my publisher Paul Dickson.

Thanks to my readers, friends, colleagues and random passers-by in the Adam and Eve pub in Norwich for their helpful suggestions, and sometimes pointing me in the right direction.

I hope you enjoy these tales as much as I have enjoyed writing them.

Peter Sargent
Norwich, September 2018

Contents

Guide to pictures in colour section

i Tilney All Saints village sign depicts the legendary Tom Hickathrift.
The Erpingham Statue at the entrance to Norwich Cathedral.

ii A cat's head was the sign of Saint Felix at Castle Rising.
The ruins of Castle Acre priory, dissolved in the 1530s.

iii The grave of Katharine of Aragon at Peterborough Cathedral.
At Lollards Pit in Norwich, unfortunate heretics were executed in the 16th Century.

iv Peacocks flaunt their plumage – much as the builders of Elizabethan Kirby Hall did.
The 1593 trial of the 'Warboys witches' is reflected on this weather vane in the Cambridgeshire village.

v Sir Robert Mansel fought a bloody duel in Norwich.
Artist Thomas Gainsborough immortalised Mr and Mrs Andrews, and the countryside around Sudbury.

vi The Clarkson Memorial in Wisbech.
A blue plaque marks the site of the White Swan, Norwich, where Victorian boxer Jem Mace was the landlord.

vii Samuel Morton Peto helped bring the railways to the east.
The Sealed Knot re-enact the Siege of Crowland.
(Picture: Rusty Aldwinckle)

viii Wartime evacuees in Norfolk, 1939.
Surviving walls at the Roman town of Venta Icenorum.

Bloodgate Fort

When the Romans invaded Britain in 43AD they found a long-settled society. But how did these people live, and where? Archaeologists and historians are gradually piecing together the puzzle – and some answers may be found at an open field in north Norfolk.

These would be the Iceni?

Well, were they? We know the Iceni were powerful in south Norfolk – but were they the same people who built a large and sophisticated 'hill fort' near what is now South Creake, north-west of Fakenham? As they left no written records, we have only educated guesswork and painstaking archaeology to go by. Up until the mid-19th century the ramparts of Bloodgate Hill had been visible for hundreds of years as a local landmark recorded in early maps. But Britain's agricultural revolution led to the area being ploughed up and levelled in 1827 as traditional field patterns were broken up. Which is ironic, as it was an earlier agricultural revolution which probably led to the fort being built in the first place. In the Iron Age, roughly by 800BC in Britain, people were using improved tools. Abandoning bronze in favour of iron meant better ploughs could bring marginal land and inferior soils into cultivation. More farming meant more food, which meant a larger population could be nurtured and sustained.

Good news all round. . .

A population explosion also meant more competition for land. Human nature and organisation being what it is, that inevitably led to armed conflict. As a species, we're not known for our tolerance of others! That was most likely the reason why Bloodgate Hill and other forts in Norfolk were built. We do not know exactly who made the fortifications here and at similar places, such as Warham Camp, Holkham, Thetford and Narborough. Were they from the same tribe, or were they in conflict with one another? Warfare would have been a relatively small scale affair, with bands descending on small farms in search of cattle and plunder, perhaps a little bit of kidnapping now and then.

The fort may have had a number of functions; a sanctuary from raiders, a place to reassure friends and awe enemies, but also may have been a religious site, a place of assembly and a market place. These Iron Age societies are something of a mystery; their religious beliefs in particular are little understood. Bloodgate Hill has impressive easterly views over the undulating Norfolk countryside of the Burn Valley, vital for spotting attackers, as well as being close enough to the sea. From about 800BC until the coming of the Romans it would have been an important local centre. Its use may well have changed over a period of nearly 1,000 years, depending on circumstances. There is little evidence of a large, settled population.

How was it built?

The manual work of many people – perhaps slave labour – would have been needed, and regular maintenance would have employed a workforce. Aerial photography and a geophysical survey have shown up the proportions of the site. Created in a circle, it was 210m (nearly 700ft) in diameter. The outer ditch was steep – about 4m (c12ft) deep – and would have been lined with wooden ramparts, probably with a walkway for sentries and loops for archers to fire through. Modern archaeology suggests there were up to three towered entrances to the fort. In the centre stood an inner rampart, with its own ditch and wooden wall. This may have been a final defensive position, a "town square", a chieftain's dwelling or a religious enclave. We can imagine neighbouring farmers and warriors from the countryside around converging there for special events and feasts. The interior may have been full of buildings and pens for horses and cattle brought in for safety during times of unrest. There is little evidence of timescale, though a cattle bone dated to 280BC has been unearthed.

'Bloodgate' suggests something rather nasty happened there. . .

Maybe. It's the name of the road leading from South Creake, and its origin is unknown. A 17th century parish map of South Creake shows the main defences, then known as 'Burgh Dykes', uncultivated and still preserved. Nor do we know if the site was occupied or defended by the time the Romans arrived in 43AD. Celtic hill forts may have been successful in warding off hostile British tribes, but against the imperial war machine they fared badly. The Romans were masters of siege warfare, employing sophisticated weaponry and tactics. First century Roman historian Tacitus describes an early attack on an unnamed Iceni fort in about 50AD (probably at Stonea, near March in Cambridgeshire), dismissing it as "an enclosure surrounded by a crude and rustic bank with a narrow entrance". It quickly fell to the Roman assault. Near Dorchester in Dorset the defenders of Maiden Castle, the largest hill fort in Europe and still an impressive site, also defied the Romans. They didn't stand a chance. The defenders were massacred – it is believed the skeletons bearing terrible injuries found by archaeologists in the 1930s were battle victims. Perhaps this early form of military terrorism intimidated the inhabitants of Bloodgate Hill into a tame surrender. Or perhaps many of them marched with Boudica of the Iceni in her famous revolt of 61AD. Sadly, it's all speculation, and likely to remain so. What is certain is that the site was abandoned by the 1st century AD.

And the modern day?

There's little to see at Bloodgate Hill now, though it's set in a particularly fine part of the north Norfolk countryside. The area became briefly famous during the early 1930s when the landowners were among the first to go over to full agricultural mechanisation – the Alley brothers ditching horses and many workers in favour of tractors. The Norfolk Archaeological Trust bought the site in 2003 and conducted a full geophysical survey, which showed up many fascinating insights. Aerial photography also demonstrated the contours of the site, including the inner ramparts. "There are no plans to disturb the site by excavating it further for the moment, but the artist's reconstruction could be used one day as a model in a carefully planned excavation to test theories about the layout of the interior," says the Trust on its website. Perhaps Bloodgate Hill will release more of its secrets in the future?

Go to www.norfarchtrust.org.uk for more details.
The site is cared for by the Norfolk Archaeological Trust and is open to the public, just off the South Creake to Syderstone road (OS Explorer Map 251). There are information boards and artist's recreations of what the fort may have looked like in its heyday – but visitors will need to employ their imaginations.

1st century **61AD**

Palace of the Iceni

Boudica's tribe – the Iceni – ruled most of Norfolk in the 1st century AD. A mysterious people, they left little to history but the judgment of their enemies. But the town of Thetford may hold many of their secrets.

The site of Boudica's palace?

Following their defeat by the Romans, the Iceni were nearly wiped out. Their old tribal base, in south and south-west Norfolk, was moved by the Romans to the north, and they were reinvented as Romano-British subjects of empire. With no written records, and no monumental buildings left behind, historians have struggled to build up a picture of Iron Age Britain. Much of what follows has to be based on educated guesswork and speculation. But the earliest origins of Thetford gives important pointers to the nature of Iron Age life. Thetford grew up where two rivers – the Thet and Little Ouse – met. An ancient trackway known as the Icknield Way crossed a series of fords across the rivers. This route ran from the Chiltern hills, skirted the edge of the fens, then a treacherous, inhospitable marsh, entering what is now Norfolk at Thetford. There it branched off in two directions; towards the north-west and the Lincolnshire Wolds, and towards the north-east. Of three main fords, one stood at what is now Thetford's Town Bridge and another two at Nuns Bridge. There must have been plenty of people on the move, as there was a great deal of trade going on in Iron Age Britain, a land that was rich in minerals. Industry in the shape of flint mining went on nearby at Grimes Graves for several centuries from about 2500BC, evidence of a fairly sophisticated society. Historians believe the name of the later town came from an Old English term – Theod-ford – the 'people's ford'. Long before the arrival of the English, though, a Celtic people held sway. They were the Iceni.

A powerful tribe?

The Iceni ruled most of what became Norfolk, plus north Suffolk, and their influence extended into Cambridgeshire. They were wealthy, known as skilled metalworkers who loved horses for both sport and war. The area around

Breckland was the Iceni heartland, reflected in place names such as Ickworth, Icklington, Ixworth and Ickburgh. In about 500BC they constructed a hillfort at Thetford to guard the fords and trackways. 'Hillfort' is a rather misleading term; it was only slightly elevated but stood on an excellent site, at the top of a low ridge commanding views in all directions and along the valleys. It remains at the heart of the town, and was later adapted by the Normans. Archaeology suggests the fort was extended and improved by the Iceni about 40 years before the Roman invasion. Two big ditches, 30ft wide and 16ft deep with vertical sides and a flat bottom deterred attack, and it likely they were augmented by rows of sharpened stakes. The most likely enemies of the 1st century Iceni were their neighbours, the Trinovantes, or the Belgae people of the south. But a far more potent threat had its eyes on the riches of Britannia.

The Romans!

Following the invasion of 43AD the Iceni did well at first. King Prasutagus allied himself with the invaders. Shortly before the invasion, an elaborate building was constructed at Thetford. At what is now Gallows Hill an 11-acre wooden enclosure with a system of fences led to a complex of three large, circular wooden buildings and a D-shaped building. The construction could contain many people, but it was neither a fort nor a centre of population. It seems likely this was either a religious site or a royal palace. Built to impress, there is evidence of coins being minted there – a royal mint? Perhaps this was one of a number of royal establishments. In 61AD Prasutagus died, and his widow Boudica was at the mercy of the imperial power. The Romans moved in to take control. According to legend, the queen was flogged and her daughters raped. Did these outrages happen at the Thetford palace? And was it here that Boudica rallied her people to take their revenge? The annals are irritatingly vague about locations. Some have suggested the site at Cockley Cley, near Swaffham, as a likelier location. The Iceni and their Trinovantes allies destroyed Roman towns at Colchester, London and St Albans before their comprehensive defeat in the midlands. Boudica died, probably by suicide, and her people tasted imperial retribution. The site at Gallows Hill was deliberately destroyed; levelled so that all traces vanished. The site of Thetford remained important, even though the Romans built a military road – the Peddars Way – some miles to the east. It seems the natives continued to use Icknield Way. There is no evidence of a town during Roman times, though some have suggested there may have been a settlement called Sitomagus.

1st century **70AD**

Rome makes its mark

For centuries Norwich has been the undisputed capital of Norfolk. But in Roman times you would have to travel a little further south to find the region's most important settlement. Caistor St Edmund is the site where the Iceni of Roman Britain flourished for more than three centuries.

The Iceni – Boudica's tribe

For the Iceni, Boudica's defeat and subsequent harsh imperial reprisals were the end of an era. Their main tribal centre, probably at Thetford, was destroyed; from now on they would be thoroughly Romanised. For the ordinary country people it might not have made much difference. Unless a Roman villa was built on their land, as at Brancaster or what's now Castle Rising, they would have carried on farming and living as before. For those who gravitated to the town, life changed. Venta Icenorum, the marketplace of the Iceni, was founded about ten years after Boudica's rebellion. Recent evidence indicates it had been an Iceni settlement before the Roman incursion. This may be the reason the town evolved at this site, rather than the more obvious one which became Norwich centuries later. It's possible the Roman army took over the site following Boudica's rebellion, and the town emerged in more peaceful times. Just one of the many questions which need answering. It seems the gridiron street plan dates to the period after 70AD. Within a century Venta was a flourishing centre of trade, religion and politics.

There's little to see now

Sadly, virtually nothing remains of the town, only some fragments of the once imposing later wall and ramparts. But archaeology enables us to picture the scene as it was – though it takes a little imagination. Built on the banks of the River Tas, the founders made best use of the situation for trade and communications. Some of the roads built to link Venta with the rest of Roman Britain have formed the foundations of current highways, such as the A140, while trains can be seen from the site. The river would also have been useful for sanitation. Trade with continental Europe flourished, with imports such as wine and pottery coming in at the port near modern Yarmouth, ferried inland by river and unloaded at a quay next to the town. Exports included corn. Sheltering under the peace and order of the empire the town grew, and had a basilica (equivalent of a town hall), two temples within the walls (and it seems one outside), public baths and an ampitheatre for the citizens to enjoy sophisticated Roman entertainments.

How do we know so much from so little?

In 1929 aerial photography during a drought showed up the outlines of the town. Extensive excavation followed, showing plenty of evidence of the development of Venta. The main building materials used in the town were flint, red tile, unfired clay and wood. A bronze saucepan handle, decorated with a figure of the god Mercury, may have been associated with one of the pagan temples, while the town was an industrial centre. Evidence to date has been found for production of glass, bronze brooches, woollen yarn and pottery. A blue glass cup, decorated with a chariot race scene, may reflect the kind of sports people enjoyed at the large oval arena on the outskirts of town. Meanwhile, river dredging uncovered a curse scratched in lead asking for the help of the river god to catch a thief and return some stolen items. Roman and British cultures eventually merged over the years as the plan to Romanise the Iceni began to work.

What about the walls? If the colony was so secure why were they so necessary?

For a century defences were not necessary, and this was probably Venta's golden age. But from about 200AD onwards raiders from northern Europe, themselves pressurised by land-hungry peoples from the east, began attacking the coast of Britain. Wealthy Venta would have been a prime target for sea-borne attackers – and the townspeople had to protect themselves. Their defences were impressive, with walls 23 feet (7m) high, taller than the remains seen today. At the base the walls are 14 feet (4m) thick. A walkway protected by a parapet ran along the top of the wall. A large ditch 80 feet (24.4m) wide by 17 feet (5m) deep was dug around the outside of the walls on three sides. This joined with the river to form a ring of defence around the town. Impressions have been found left by the studs of a hobnailed boot embedded in mortar, which probably belonged to one of the workers. Four large guarded gateways commanded entrances to the town. At the same time sea defences were beefed up at Caister and Burgh Castle (on the east coast) and Brancaster to the north-west.

It didn't work in the long run

Overstretched, and threatened at home, imperial rule faltered. It seems likely that mercenaries were hired from among the very Saxon, Angle and Jute peoples who were attacking the colony, many of whom stayed. Early in the fifth century the legions were withdrawn, the invaders moved in – and Britannia eventually became England. Historians are divided as to how it happened, some claiming the assimilation was more peaceful than hitherto thought. Towns like Venta and Brancaster were abandoned. From the middle of the fifth century Venta began its long decay. Buildings and walls alike were dismantled and used for local construction. The Saxons who settled in East Anglia knew the site as Caister – based on the Latin word for camp, 'castra' – and the name stuck. Several hundred years later a church was founded within the original walls (was there an original Roman church there?) dedicated to Saint Edmund and using tiles from the Roman town. It has been in use for 900 years.

And today?

In 1984 the site passed to the Norfolk Archaeological Trust. Conservation work began and it was opened to the public in 1993. Today it is managed in partnership with South Norfolk Council. Work is ongoing at the site, and new discoveries are being made, which will no doubt alter the view of the town and its history. To see a Roman town where more buildings survived you have to travel to Wroxeter, near Shrewsbury in the west midlands.

Caistor Roman town is four miles south of Norwich, near Stoke Holy Cross. Entry is free. It's a beautiful site, popular with dog walkers. Pictured right is a surviving fragment of the walls.

1st century **61AD**

The Legionary Way

The Peddars Way is popular with ramblers and cyclists. It is part of a national trail of long distance paths that those who want to leave the modern world of speedy communications behind them for a while enjoy. But for what reason was it originally built?

A road to nowhere?

A route from south to north, ending abruptly at the north Norfolk coast. The late Bruce Robinson, author of the guide to the Peddars Way, described it as a "road with no beginning, no certainty, and no end". What was the point? The answer seems to lie 2,000 years in the past, with the Roman army. The Peddars Way – the name itself is medieval – is a 46-mile-long (74km) path from Knettishall Heath in Suffolk's Brecklands to Holme-next-the-Sea in west Norfolk, linked for modern use to the even more popular Norfolk Coast Path. To unravel the mystery we must forget our own time, when people walk for health or pleasure, and return to an era when travelling across England was difficult, particularly if you wanted to conquer the country. Lines of communication in the area date back to the Bronze Age thousands of years ago. The ancient Icknield Way links the west country with East Anglia; in places it runs parallel with the later Peddars Way. By the 1st century AD the region was dominated by the Iceni tribe. After their uprising led by Boudicca, and subsequent crushing defeat, the Roman conquerors set themselves the task of 'pacifying' Norfolk and Suffolk.

The right to Rome?

The Iceni powerbase was in what is now west Norfolk and Suffolk; it was through this homeland that the Romans built their new road. It was a "text-book Roman road, driven across country without regard to native features". No doubt they needed a fast, all-weather road for their legions. But why did it finish at Holme? Modern historians have concluded there was probably a ferry to take them across The Wash, which was then far narrower than it is now. That would give them an alternative route from centres such as London,

Chelmsford and Colchester to the north – linking their major military bases at Lincoln and York – to the existing Ermine Street, now the Great North Road (A1). Perhaps there was another motive. The road cut through Iceni territory and emphasised to the conquered people that the legions were here to stay, and that they had better get used to the fact; it would have been an impressive construction. Roman engineering was the wonder of the age. They surveyed their route meticulously, laid a bottom layer of large stones, then covered it with a surface of rammed flint, creating famously straight highways complete with effective drainage. They built at least one bridge, over the River Thet in the south. It is easy to imagine prisoners taken after Boudicca's defeat pressed into building it. Its military character is illustrated by the fact no major habitations developed there, apart from Castle Acre near modern Swaffham, although there is evidence of a number of Romano-British villas to the west of the road. The Romans developed a site further to the east, near modern Norwich, which grew into into a major town, as we saw in the previous chapter.

What did the Romans ever do for us?

Apart from the roads, they brought peace. After the crushing of Boudicca's revolt, much of the southern province of Britannia settled down to a period of relative harmony and prosperity within the Empire. It was over a century before external threats led to coastal forts being built along the 'Saxon Shore' – at places like Brancaster, a little east of Holme, Caister and Burgh Castle, near modern day Great Yarmouth. Peddars Way, known to the Romans as Limes Icenorum, did not go out of use when the Empire fell. In the 11th century it was the site of a Danish victory when a Norse leader named Thorkell beat an

Rome free: A signpost along the Peddars Way.

English force under Ealdorman Ulfcytell, probably at East Wretham near Thetford. During medieval times it gradually became known as the 'Pedlar's Way', meaning a 'foot' road. Another possible derivation of the name is that it came from 'ped', a wicker basket used for carrying goods. The road's use fluctuated through centuries of economic rise and fall. After the arrival of the Normans it was on the pilgrim trail to the shrine at Walsingham, and no doubt got a boost from being used by these devout travellers, many of whom would have stopped off at convenient places such as Castle Acre priory. As late as the 17th century it was still marked on maps as a major route. The Royalist Le Strange family of Hunstanton, who opposed Oliver Cromwell's Parliamentarians during the Civil War and briefly captured King's Lynn in 1643, stockpiled arms and ammunition at a still-standing store on the road at Sedgeford, south of Holme. At Fring it formed the parish boundary as late as 1901, but the coming of the railways and better roads in the 19th century finally killed it off.

Until the modern day

The walk was added to a national trail covering much of southern England in 1986, along with the newly created Norfolk Coast Path, in a ceremony performed by the Prince of Wales at Holme-next-the-Sea. My Lonely Planet Walking in Britain guide book rather sniffily dismisses the Way as "not the most interesting of routes", but this is surely unfair. The trail begins in the heaths of the Brecks, goes through rolling farmland and hills that belie Norfolk's flat reputation, and ends in the outstanding beauty of the coast. You travel through woodland and heath; at Thompson, near the start of the walk, you can see pingo ponds, said to be formed during the last Ice Age. As well as Castle Acre, the route goes through the villages of Little Cressingham and Ringstead, but otherwise it is pure country walking. In some sections it feels like you are in a land that time forgot. There are some 'lost' sections, and part of the route is on lanes used by traffic and you have to cross two major roads, but you get to see much of the variety of the area's landscape in easy and tranquil walking conditions – as well as imagine you are marching with a Roman legion.

Anything else?

One last thing. The Peddars Way is said to be among the many haunts of East Anglia's spooky spectral 'devil' dog of ancient legend – Black Shuck.

7th century **630AD**

Spreading the faith

The Christian faith was established in eastern England in the seventh century AD – when East Anglia was an independent kingdom. Kings, saintly princesses and bishops led the way to making this a Christian country.

England wasn't quite England yet. . .

What is now England comprised several warring kingdoms; Wessex, Kent, Northumbria, Mercia in the midlands – and East Anglia. It's hard to feel complete confidence in the history of this period. Few records were kept, and many ecclesiastical documents were later destroyed by Viking raiders. Places, names and dates are debatable. Most of our knowledge comes from Bede, the Jarrow monk of Northumbria, whose Ecclesiastical History of the English People was written a century after the events related here. We know the Anglo-Saxon people settled in these lands by about 600AD were pagans. Although Christianity was not unknown in these islands, it was centred upon Ireland and among the Britons of the west. In East Anglia, the early 600s saw the kingdom at its most powerful; King Raedwald, a member of the Wuffing dynasty, was acknowledged as 'Bretwalda' – overlord – of southern Britain. Eastern England had strong links to the continent. Trade brought wealth, as can be seen in the grave goods in the Sutton Hoo site, near Woodbridge. Today it is widely believed Raedwald was the man buried there.

Christian or pagan?

The Dark Ages emerge from legend into the pages of history in 597. Saint Augustine was sent by Pope Gregory the Great in Rome to convert the English to Christianity. (The tale goes he saw some blond English children being sold as slaves in Rome. Being told they were Angles, he responded they were 'not Angles, but angels'). Augustine made instant headway at the Kentish court. It helped that Queen Bertha, a French princess, was already Christian. She and Augustine – 'Apostle to the English' – converted King Aethelbert to the faith, along with other nobles. Among them was Raedwald, visiting from East

Anglia. Baptism may have been a political move on Raedwald's part – the Christian God a new, powerful, albeit phenomenally hard-working deity, one of many he felt the need to placate. Whatever his views, it was his son Sigbert who became the key player. Succeeding to the East Anglian throne, he encouraged Christianity in his lands. Soon he was looking for a man to spread the word.

A job with prospects. . .

Felix, later sainted, was a priest from Burgundy in what is now France. Invited by Sigbert, he arrived in 630, and spent the rest of his life on a mission to convert the English. He was pushing at an open door, especially with the nobility. Sigbert appointed him Bishop of East Anglia and gave him a site at Dommoc. There is dispute about where this was; some say it was Dunwich, the Suffolk port which has long since disappeared under the waves. Others maintain Dommoc was actually Walton Castle, near Felixstowe. This was a former Roman fort which historians such as Dr Sam Newton think was adapted and re-used by Christians. This view is reinforced by evidence at Burgh Castle, near Great Yarmouth. Also a one-time Roman fortress, it was settled as a mission by the Irish Saint Fursey around the same time. The walls would have given protection to the bishop, while proximity to Roman roads and a safe harbour were useful for communications. It would be nice to claim 'Felixstowe' was named after the saint, but this too is disputed.

Complicated, these Dark Ages. . .

Wherever he was based, Bishop Felix was making progress, preaching and converting. "In no part of England was Christianity more favourably introduced," wrote Bede – and coming from a Northumbrian that's praise indeed. Felix concentrated on education, influencing the next generation. "Desiring to imitate those things which he had seen well arranged in Gaul, he founded a school in which boys might be taught letters, Felix, the bishop. . . furnished them with masters, after the Kentish fashion." He also founded an important monastery at Soham in Cambridgeshire. Heading north by sea, Felix reached Norfolk. He is

Felix 'the cat': St Felix's symbol can be seen at Castle Rising in Norfolk.

associated with the Castle Rising area, near King's Lynn on the coast. Arriving at the now lost port of Babingley, he founded a church (the ruins remain) and made conversions. In a mostly illiterate age his symbol was a cat – Felix is Latin for 'cat' – and this can be seen carved in the walls at Castle Rising. One far-fetched legend maintains he was rescued from drowning in the River Babingley by beavers, and consequently made their leader a bishop.

Christianity established then, peace and harmony all round . . .
England was rarely at peace. In neighbouring Mercia, King Penda was still pagan. He had his own issues with East Anglia, which was expanding west into his lands via the Fens. Penda invaded. Sigbert had retired to a monastery. Begged by his subjects to lead them into battle, he reluctantly did so, armed only with a stick. Defeated, he was killed and became Christian East Anglia's first martyr. His successor King Anna (confusing, these Saxon names) was even more devout, while his daughters became famous for their piety. Inspired by Felix, Etheldreda founded the nunnery at Ely, Withberga performed miracles at Dereham and Seaxburga and Aethelburga also made their mark. Etheldreda, also known as Audrey, inspired an annual medieval fair at Ely. Known as St Audrey's Fair, it featured the sale of lace necklaces. In later years these were seen as cheap and gaudy – hence the word 'tawdry'. High status females often led the way in conversion to Christianity. In 2017, the remains of an aristocratic woman were unearthed at Winfarthing, near Diss. The find, by a then UEA student, which made national headlines, uncovered a two gold pendants in the form of a Maltese cross. These indicated the woman buried there was a Christian. The burial has been dated at c650-675AD. Recent archaeological work at Reedham, near Yarmouth, meanwhile, shows that the Christian church there was built on the remains of a small Roman fortress dating from the third or fourth centuries. The Christian faith was already strong in East Anglia by the time Felix died in 647. But disaster soon struck again. That persistent Penda came east, and killed Anna and his son in a battle believed to have been fought near Blythburgh in Suffolk. Fursey's monastery at Castle Burgh was also sacked, prompting the saint to sail for France and safety. Penda's eventual defeat and death at the hands of Christian Northumbria settled religious matters. The East Anglian see was eventually divided in two, with the Norfolk headquarters at North Elmham, Suffolk's at Dommoc. Monasteries and churches thrived until the Vikings arrived in the 860s. But that's another story.

8th century **700s**

The saga of Beowulf

***Paet wae god cyning* (He was a good king). So an eighth century poet writing in early English described the mythical hero Beowulf – but where was this epic written?**

Beowulf? Viking hero, wasn't he?

Certainly not a Viking. He was a proper English hero. The stirring tale of Beowulf is the first surviving work written in Old English. The only known manuscript dates from the 10th century, but the tale harks back to an even earlier age. Close examination suggests the mythology contained within it may derive from East Anglia, meaning it could be from this region. Although the action is set in Scandinavia, it was written for an English audience.

What's it about?

Beowulf is a tale of adventure, monsters and warriors. The hero – an aristocrat of the Geat people of Sweden – sails with his warriors to fifth century Denmark to rid this kingdom of a monster, who has repeatedly attacked King Hrothgar's hall and terrorised his people. The creature is Grendel, a half-human, half-supernatural being who hates mankind with a vengeance. Beowulf and his men sleep in the royal hall, awaiting Grendel. Sure enough, that night he arrives. Beowulf fights him with his bare hands, ripping off his arm and mortally wounding him. Beowulf nails the arm to the hall door as a mark of triumph. The monster slinks away, and dies of his wounds. But he has a mother, and she is worse than Grendel. With a mother's grief, but a monster's ferocity, she launches a deadly attack on the humans. Beowulf tracks her to her marshy lair and kills her too following a fierce fight, this time with a giant's sword. He returns to a hero's welcome. Fifty years pass, and Beowulf has become king in his native Sweden. But then a new enemy arrives; this time in the form of a fire-breathing fifty-foot long dragon laying waste to the kingdom after the treasure he was guarding has been stolen. The ageing king Beowulf, accompanied by just one young warrior, prepares for one last battle with the dragon. Knowing he is doomed to die, the hero does not hesitate. He eventually manages to kill the dragon, but is himself slain. His grieving people give him a magnificent cremation on board a ship, and the tale ends.

What's it got to do with East Anglia?

If the tale sounds familiar, it is because it has been imitated and repeated in books and films since. Anglo-Saxon historian Dr Sam Newton, in his Origins of Beowulf, suggests the poem was devised in the early eighth century, most likely in Suffolk, during the reign of King Aelfward. East Anglia, comprising most of what is now Norfolk and Suffolk, was an independent kingdom. It had strong cultural and trading links to Denmark and Sweden, its ruling house, the Wuffings, possibly related to their royal families. So the themes in Beowulf would be familiar to these early English people, many of whom would have memories of the lands from which they or their forebears had migrated. Tales like that of Beowulf, containing names of real people from Denmark and Sweden, would have struck a chord with people who had only recently settled in a new country. The poem would have been recited by a bard, no doubt to great dramatic effect in a hall presided over by a nobleman or king, and only later written down. Rendlesham in Suffolk is one site associated with the East Anglian kings, and a possible candidate for the spot where Beowulf was composed.

What about Grendel?

The characters of Grendel and his mother may have their roots in East Anglia. To the early English the fens were uncharted territory – "uninhabitable country" – as the Beowulf poet writes. When the eighth century Saint Guthlac built his monastery at Crowland in the fens, he wrote darkly of being haunted by demons and monsters, the 'seed of Cain' and enemies of mankind living in the marshy fens. Such a demon is Grendel, so an East Anglian poet may have added this supernatural character to the mix. ". . . an enemy from hell. Grendel they called this cruel spirit, the fell and fen his fastness was, the marsh his haunt. This unhappy being had long lived in the land of monsters since the Creator cast them out as kindred of Cain." Beowulf dives into a murky mere to fight Grendel's mother; maybe the poet had the waterlands of the fens in mind when he wrote this part. A more modern character may be linked to the story. In Old English a 'scucca' means 'demon' – and the figure of Black Shuck, the devil dog of East Anglian lore who we met easrlier on

Peddars Way, looms large in local legend to this day. He is said to haunt the byways of Norfolk and Suffolk. Anyone who sees him is doomed to die within the year. Could the two be linked? The poem never goes into great detail as to Grendel's appearance, and there may have been a canine element to him and his mother.

What else links the legend to England?

At Sutton Hoo, near Woodbridge in Suffolk, the East Anglians carried out ship burials in the early eighth century. They have echoes of Beowulf's death and funeral. "Build me a splendid mound on the headland," orders Beowulf to his surviving warriors with his dying words, "it shall be a reminder to my people so that seafarers will call it Beowulf's Barrow". Standing at the head of the estuary of the River Deben, that is just the effect the Sutton Hoo builders had in mind, as it would have been visible to all ships arriving in England. As we saw in the last chapter, it is believed the man honoured by the magnificent ship burial unearthed in 1939 was King Raedwald of East Anglia – the kind of man in whose hall Beowulf would have been first told.

How did we get hold of the story?

We do not know who wrote Beowulf. The manuscript was one of few to survive the Viking attacks of the ninth century onwards. It also narrowly survived an 18th century fire at its home at Ashburnham Abbey, near Westminster Abbey. So its author and previous history are a matter of conjecture. Most likely it emanated from one of the great monasteries of England, many of which were in East Anglia. The fenland was home to a number of monasteries; Ely, Crowland, Ramsey and Bury St Edmunds, which were founded by the Saxons, and were islands of learning. These were the places that spawned the scholars who wrote this kind of poetry. Although the story is set in a pre-Christian age it would have appealed to an audience with a vivid memory of these pagan days and fond folk memories of ancestral lands. A number of authorities on this period of history have entered the debate on Beowulf's origins, and there are many different theories as to its provenance. J R R Tolkien, famed for his Lord of the Rings books, was one of the first to suggest it was written in the 700s. Poet Seamus Heaney's 1999 translation put it in the public eye, while the 2007 3D animated fantasy film, with an oddly cast Ray Winstone in the title role, brought Beowulf to a new audience.

10th century **917**

The birth of England

Many people submitted to King Edward, from both East Anglia and Essex, which had been under Danish rule.

This entry in the Anglo-Saxon Chronicle for 917AD marks the moment East Anglia rejoined a rapidly unifying England.

Why did it need uniting?

England had never hitherto been a single country under one ruler. The Angles and Saxons who had migrated to the island during the period which saw the collapse of the Roman Empire organised themselves into a series of competing kingdoms. On the eve of the Viking invasions Wessex, home of the 'West Saxons', was the most powerful, but Mercia, Kent, Northumbria and East Anglia had their own kings. Scandinavian Vikings from Denmark overran first Northumbria, then East Anglia by 870. East Anglian King Edmund was defeated in battle, then killed, and subsequently venerated as a saint. His kingdom came under Danish control. The Danes moved on into Mercia and the midlands, conquering most of the kingdom and threatening Wessex, the last English kingdom still standing. Belatedly, the English found a hero. Alfred, later dubbed The Great, fought the invaders to a standstill in a series of desperate battles in the late 870s, and comprehensively defeated them at Edington in Wiltshire.

Why wasn't that the end of the Norse invasion?

There was more than one Norse army in England, and many had already settled in the north and east, putting down roots as farmers and traders. The leader of the defeated army, Guthrum the Dane, accepted a truce with Alfred which saw him become the effective king of East Anglia. At Alfred's insistence he was baptised into the Christian faith as 'Athelstan', had coins minted in his name and ruled until his death in 890. The area north of London and east of the 'Five Boroughs' – Stamford, Leicester, Derby, Lincoln and Nottingham – was Danish East Anglia. We know a lot about this era as the momentous events were recorded in the Anglo-Saxon Chronicle, compiled by anonymous clerics. In 880, the Chronicle, which referred to all invading Norsemen whether Swedes, Danes or Norwegians as 'the force', recorded: "The force went into East Anglia, occupied the land and shared it out". There is no suggestion there was mass migration from Scandinavia, as had earlier taken place from the lands in Germany and the Netherlands which supplied the Anglo-Saxons. Those Scandinavian warriors who turned their swords into ploughs were relatively few in number, and it is most likely they rubbed along reasonably well with their English subjects after the initial shock of invasion. There was no question of any methodical 'ethnic cleansing' that we see in modern wars, otherwise the land would have been dangerously under-populated. The Norsemen had a gift for assimilation wherever they settled.

What was Alfred's plan?

The far-seeing Alfred was probably already dreaming of a united England (or Angleland) – under a Wessex king, of course – which would be strong enough to resist the invaders. He began building a series of forts – these 'burghs' were later known as boroughs – and also created an English navy to counter the invaders' dominance at sea. Alfred then began the reconquest. In 885, for example, he "sent a ship-force from Kent into East Anglia. . . the Danes had the victory". Unfortunately for Alfred, the Vikings were still kings of the sea. On land things were evening up. The following year he retook London after a bloody battle. "All the English turned to him, except those who were in the captivity of the Danes," wrote the Chronicle. Increasingly frustrated, the Vikings began raiding in France and the Netherlands where pickings were proving easier.

It was slow going though

The English fightback initiated by Alfred took decades to complete. The Danes held sway in the east and north, in the area known as the Danelaw. While Guthrum's headquarters were at Cambridge, Danes settled elsewhere in the east. In Norwich, for example, excavations indicate Vikings settled in numbers, many as traders, and thrived for several generations. Many followed Guthrum's example and converted to Christianity. Although the Scandinavian presence was felt more strongly in the north, where their occupation lasted far longer, here in the east it had a lasting legacy reflected particularly in surviving place names. If you live in a place with a -by ending (eg Filby) it may have a Scandinavian origin, meaning a farm or a village. A -thorpe ending (eg Bowthorpe) indicates a small village or settlement. Similarly, the place name endings -gil, -holm, -thwaite or -toft also indicate Scandinavian origins. Despite setbacks and counter-offensives, Alfred's strategy began to work. When Viking ships from Northumbria and East Anglia raided the Wessex shore in 896 the ageing Alfred ordered longships built. "They were nearly twice as long as the others," wrote the Chronicle, "they were both swifter and steadier". The English were learning the hard way. The tide was turning.

Alfred couldn't carry on forever

The king died in 900. His son Edward inherited his crown, while his impressive warrior daughter Aethelflaed had married the king of Mercia, turning a former rival into an ally. Known as 'the Lady of the Mercians' she was at the forefront of the English fightback. Alfred's children carried on their father's work, and proved worthy successors. The English were pressing the Danelaw from all sides; the Mercians from the midlands, where frontier fortresses such as Stamford became important, and north from London and Essex. The climax came in 917 when Danes from East Anglia advanced from Huntingdon and built a fort at Tempsford, now on the route of the A1 south of St Neots. Local English forces under Edward were joined by men from Kent, Surrey and Essex. This army stormed the fort, killing many Danish leaders. They were on the offensive now, and seized Colchester and Maldon in Essex. East Anglia's Vikings capitulated. "All the people of the area around Huntingdon who had survived bowed to King Edward, and sought his peace and protection," reported the Chronicle ". . .all the force in East Anglia swore an agreement to do all he wished, to keep the peace with all the king kept peace with, both on sea and on land. The force belonging to Cambridge chose him especially as lord and protector, and affirmed it with oaths as he determined it."

No more fighting then!

Vikings north of the Humber were in no mood to surrender. English forces, joined by those of East Anglia, marched steadily north. A generation passed before the England we recognise today was fully unified under Athelstan, Alfred's grandson – and even then there was more fighting to do as they came into conflict with the Scots, Welsh and Irish.

11th century **1066**

The fenland giant

In Tilney All Saints churchyard a large stone grave is just about visible. A modern sign tells us that 'Hickathrift' is buried there. But who was Hickathrift, did he really exist – and is he buried there?

Big chap, was he?

Tom Hickathrift, the fenland giant, was, as the name implies, somewhat out of the ordinary. His tale is inextricably linked to the marshland villages between King's Lynn and Wisbech. But his exploits, like those of Robin Hood and other folklore heroes, such as Hereward the Wake, have become so enmeshed in legend and tall tales that it is too late to know truth from fiction. Tom has been linked to heroes of myth, such as Jack and the Beanstalk, heroes of reality such as Richard the Lionheart and William the Conqueror – and gods of the Celts and Vikings. We can be sure of little, but perhaps the tales are based on some form of reality.

Myth or man?

The story goes that Tom lived in the remote marshland at Tilney before, or during, the reign of William the Conqueror (ruled 1066-87). That's the version as written down for the first time in the 17th century, but it had been handed down by word of mouth for several centuries previously, and had no doubt been embellished. Stories such as this were passed on via chapbooks, small paper pamphlets sold by travelling pedlars. The most popular version of the legend goes like this. The son of a farm labourer, Tom was a gentle, but idle, giant. Not overfond of work, he would sit at home and eat large meals, "as much as would serve four or five ordinary men". He was indulged by his widowed mother. "So much did he grow that when he was but ten years old he was already eight feet high, and his hand like a shoulder of mutton." It was time to go to work. Tom's first feat of strength came while working the land, when he carried some 20 hundredweight of straw over his shoulder, more than 20 men could carry. Tom's fame spread, and he drew admiring crowds at local fairs. "At cudgels, wrestling or throwing the hammer, not a man could stand against him." His football skills were legendary, kicking the ball so hard "that it flew none could tell whither". A later version said he once kicked a ball from Beccles to Bungay, though this Suffolk location takes him away from his usual fenland patch. His strength could be a double-edged weapon. On one occasion he joined in a football game, and kicked the ball so far it was lost. The other players rounded on him, whereupon Tom "walked across to a nearby house that had collapsed in a recent storm, picked up a beam and began to lay about him. All that got in the way he either killed or stunned." He was in danger of becoming a bully.

Time to pick on someone his own size. . .

A fearsome giant lived in the marsh between Lynn and Wisbech, robbing and murdering travellers. A Lynn brewer needed to get his beer to Wisbech, and hired Tom to take it through the marshes. He promised him "a new suit of clothes from top to toe, and that he should eat and drink of the best". Tom was fond of his beer, so took the job. The brewer told him to take the long way round, and avoid the giant's lair. But Tom found the journey of about 20 miles too long. Without telling anyone else, he took the brewer's horse and cart the short cut via The Smeeth, an area of pastureland in the marshes, even though he knew the giant lived in a cave there. The ogre emerged, "12ft tall and 6ft about the waist", carrying a huge club, "intending to dash out Tom's brains at the first blow". He demanded Tom's beer, threatening to hang his head on a nearby tree if he did not hand it over. A number of other severed heads already hung there. Hickathrift was not afraid. "A fig in your teeth," he told the giant. "You shall not find me like one of them, traitorly rogue that you are." With that, the two fought an epic battle to the death. Improvising for weapons, Tom turned his cart upside down and used the axle-tree and wheel for a sword and shield. After a fierce fight he killed the giant. He cut off his head, seized his stolen treasure in the cave – "a great store of silver and gold which made his heart leap" – and went on to Wisbech.

Popular winner?

Tom was an instant hero. "All the folk made bonfires for joy, and if Tom was respected before, he was much more so now." As the man who had made the marshland safe for travellers he became a local celebrity. Where the giant's cave had stood he built himself a fine house, and granted poor people grazing rights nearby. "Now he became the chief man in the countryside, 'twas no longer plain Tom, but Mr Hickathrift. . . he kept men and maids, made him a park to keep deer, and time passed with him happily to the end of his days." Some versions go further, maintaining the king knighted Tom and made him governor of Thanet in Kent.

Any truth in it?

Various traditions link Tom Hickathrift with the marshland villages around King's Lynn, so it's possible the legends are based on a real person. Was there a local strongman who rid the marshes of bandits and was generous to the poor? He would certainly have been well-liked. Many feats of strength or oddity in the region, regardless of historical accuracy, have been attributed to Hickathrift. At Walpole St Peter near Tilney, for example, a dent in the ground is said to be where a cannonball landed after Tom threw it there to scare away the devil. The oldest surviving version of the Hickathrift legend in print was in a book of the 1660s, a time when oral myths were being codified and recorded. The modern version quoted here was tidied up by Australian 19th century folklorist Joseph Jacobs in an anthology of English fairy tales. Jacobs also brought familiar tales such as Jack and the Beanstalk, Goldilocks and the three bears and The History of Tom Thumb to life. Recent historians have read a lot more into Hickathrift's legend. There are a number of theories. Some say that Hickathrift is really based on an ancient Celtic sun god, Hwicce, or perhaps even an Anglo-Saxon version of the Scandinavian god Thor, he of the mighty lightning and thunderbolts and gargantuan appetite. The Tom as related in our tale seems a more down-to-earth character than that. Another theory links him to a Norman knight and local landowner named Frederick de Tylney, or Baron of Tylney. Frederick, a powerful champion said to be unusually tall, accompanied King Richard I, the 'Lionheart', on his Crusade in the late 1100s – and died at the siege of Acre in the Middle East. Readers may prefer the giant-killing, football-kicking Tom of the original, home-grown legend. At Tilney All Saints Tom is pictured on the village sign with the cartwheel he used to defeat the giant. The gravestone can be seen close to the church in Tilney All Saints with a modern printed sign next to it. According to some accounts, an axle-tree and cartwheel once figured on a stone tomb there. Is this the resting place of the fenland giant?

Revolt of the earls

The Normans built Norwich Castle soon after the conquest of 1066. It was not long before its defences were put to the test.

An English fightback?

By 1075 most English resistance had been crushed. Hereward the Wake's fenland guerrilla campaign had been defeated when the Isle of Ely fell, the rebellious north had been harried mercilessly – but William the Conqueror's kingdom was still not secure. Now though the threat came from within, when men he believed were loyal to him made to seize his crown. They were led by Ralph Guader, Earl of East Anglia, from his new castle at Norwich.

Who was Earl Ralph?

Ralph de Guader was of Breton descent, born in about 1042. His father was referred to as an Englishman. It is more likely he was a Frenchman who had settled in England for a while. It is possible this elder Ralph had travelled to England with Queen Emma of Normandy, who was married to English king Ethelred (aka the Unready) and later King Cnut. Legend has it the younger Ralph was born at Hereford or in Wales. As a young man he fought in a number of campaigns in France. In 1066 he and his father joined Duke William of Normandy on the greatest gamble of his career; the invasion of England. Victorious at Hastings, William's followers and allies expected – and received – the spoils of victory. In the Guaders' case, it was land in East Anglia, comprising bits of Norfolk, Suffolk and Cambridgeshire as well as land in the south, from the dispossessed English. It was most likely they who began work on the new castle at Norwich in 1067 – demolishing nearly 100 houses, according to the Domesday Book, and evicting the inhabitants – as they turned the growing town into their Norfolk capital. Three years after Hastings, the Guaders routed a force of Norse raiders – Vikings – who had invaded Norfolk and briefly occupied Norwich. In gratitude, William made the family Earls of East Anglia, and Ralph the younger also inherited estates on both sides of the English Channel following his father's death.

Right, he had to be happy with that

Sadly, no. Like a lot of ambitious medieval nobles, riches and power were not enough. Perhaps watching the daring William the Conqueror seize a whole kingdom, and rise from a duke to a king, made them think they could do the same. Ralph wanted more. Soon he was intriguing with his friend Roger de Breteuil, Earl of Hereford, and one of the few remaining English earls, Waltheof. Heir to the Northumbrian earldom, Waltheof had reluctantly sided with King William. His position was at best ambivalent as he was little more than a captive at the king's court. Ralph wanted to marry Roger's sister, Emma. This alliance would boost their power and forge a dynasty. William was having none of that, and forbade the match. They went ahead nevertheless, and used the wedding in Norwich as the occasion to hatch a plot to rebel. As well as joining forces, they sealed an alliance with a fleet of Viking longships, which was to augment the rising.

A hopeless plan – surely

The plot was botched and half-hearted from the start. Waltheof, who may have been coerced into the plan, quickly confessed to Lanfranc, the Archbishop of Canterbury. With William absent in Normandy the archbishop, along with the king's cleric brother Bishop Odo, raised an army and marched against the rebels. Also with the bishops was William of Warenne, a powerful Norman lord who held lands in Norfolk. Sources such as the Anglo-Saxon Chronicle say Hereward's English rebels, who had concluded a truce with the king, fought alongside them. Whatever the truth, it seems that a large portion of the royal army which opposed the rebels was English, composed of the fyrd, the feudal militia raised in time of crisis. They supported the Conqueror against the chaos of civil war. It was, of course, under Norman command, led by fighting Bishop Odo. Rapidly defeated in battle near Cambridge, the rebels fell back on Norwich. There Ralph left his new wife Emma to defend the new castle, while he sailed for Denmark in search of reinforcements. Eventually he returned to England with a fleet of 200 ships under Cnut and Hakon, which turned tail once William returned to England. The royal army besieged Norwich Castle. This was not the mighty stone structure of today, but a rudimentary motte and bailey construction, of wood and earth. Nevertheless, the countess and her garrison held out for three months before surrendering on good terms. She and Ralph's Bretons were given 40 days to leave the country, and did so hastily. Other rebels were not so lucky; many captured at

Cambridge had a leg cut off, while at Christmas, 1075, the Conqueror himself arrived in Norwich in a particularly vengeful mood. He had some captives mutilated by gouging out eyes.

Ouch! Well, it taught them a valuable lesson. . .
And sent a powerful message of deterrence to other rebels. William, implacable as ever, now turned on the captive earls. Roger was deprived of his lands and, according to the contemporary monk and historian Orderic Vitalis, imprisoned for life. Waltheof, despite betraying the rebellion, was executed. This last representative of the English nobility was beheaded, reputedly at Winchester. However, the Anglo-Saxon Chronicle recorded that his body was buried with great ceremony at Crowland Abbey in Lincolnshire. There a cult grew up around his relics.

And Earl Ralph?
Got away with it. He lost his earldom and English lands, but, on the plus side, he kept his life and liberty. Nor did he have his eyes gouged out, so that must have been some consolation. Joined by his wife, he returned to Brittany. There he defied William with the help of the French king, and even outlived him. In 1096 he joined William's eldest son Robert on the First Crusade to the Holy Land. Crusaders were promised pardon from their sins if they helped capture Jerusalem – and Ralph had plenty to forgive. But both he and Emma died on the dangerous road to Palestine.

What happened back in Norwich?
The castle reverted to the king, and a royal garrison was installed. A great programme of building works was undertaken, culminating in the visit at Christmas 1121 by King Henry I, youngest son of the Conqueror. Limestone was shipped in from Caen, Normandy, at great expense, and the stone keep we recognise today was largely complete by the time of Henry I's visit. At much the same time, building began on the city's new cathedral. It was a traumatic time for the inhabitants, who had seen a foreign power imposed on them as well as the rigours of a siege, but the construction of the castle and the cathedral helped cement Norwich's position as capital of Norfolk and, in time, the second city in England. By the time the city received a royal charter from Henry II in 1158 its position looked secure.

12th century **1101**

Lynn and the bishop

Bishop Herbert Losinga was a busy man. Not content with helping turn Norwich into the capital of Norfolk, in 1101 he turned his attention to the county's north-west coast. There, a collection of salt pans would one day become one of the greatest ports in England.

Worth its salt, no doubt. . .

In the Middle Ages salt was a valuable commodity, which is the origin of that old phrase 'worth its salt'. It was used to cure and preserve fish and meat, vital in the days before means of artificial refrigeration were invented. The site where Lynn now stands held valuable salt pans, and these were harvested profitably by the inhabitants. It stands at the south-eastern tip of the enormous estuary of The Wash, which in those days extended much further than it does today. In fact, the sea lapped against the shore at Wisbech, well to the south of modern King's Lynn. To the Iron Age Celts this area had been known as Lin, Lenne and Leuna, meaning 'place by the pool' or 'the place of spreading waters'. It formed part of a large, salty lake created by the draining of three rivers, the Nene, Little Ouse and Great Ouse. Human habitation had gone on here, probably for thousands of years, on a small scale, making little impact. In fact, in the late 11th century Lynn was still a smaller place than Castle Rising, a few miles to the north. An old Norfolk rhyme goes: "Rising was a sea-port where Lynn was but a marsh, Now Lynn is a sea-port town and Rising fares the worse".

How do we know what was there?

The Domesday Book, first compiled in the 1080s, 20 years after the Norman Conquest, recorded details of people who worked on the saltpans in this modest village, as well as folk engaged in farming and fishing. There was a population at what would become West Lynn, on the western side of the river, North Lynn, Bishop's Lynn and South Lynn, which was regarded as a village. By the mid-1000s Lynn was composed of a group of low-lying islands between the rivers. At high tides the islands would flood with seawater, and it was here the production of salt took place. Salted sand was put in containers and salt water was passed through it. This solution was placed in vats and boiled over peat fires until the salt crystallised. Over many years discarded sand and general rubbish was thrown behind the salterns, and the land level rose. This created dry land between the Millfleet and Purfleet ('fleet' was an old Saxon name for a stream). Here were the origins of the medieval town. Eventually these 'fleets' would be filled in, recalled only by their names.

What about the bishop?

Herbert Losinga had been appointed Bishop of East Anglia after the Norman Conquest, and moved his see (headquarters) from Thetford to Norwich in 1094. He made his mark like no other local churchman, before or since. An energetic man, he was the guiding spirit behind the building of Norwich Cathedral from 1096, and also helped develop what would become another great trading town of the future – Great Yarmouth – on the east coast of Norfolk. The great wealth of the church emanated from its land; it held vast tracts throughout East Anglia. Among its manors was Gaywood, now a suburb of Lynn. There, some tenants, many of whom were salt producers, asked Losinga to found a town and grant it commercial privileges, plus build a parish church. For the bishop it was a chance to foster the growth of trade in the area around The Wash, something he did elsewhere in East Anglia. The bishop had an even more pressing need to build churches. Earlier in his career he had been found guilty of the obscure-sounding ecclesiastic sin of 'simony' – holding more than one office. This once common practice, highly lucrative for the holder, became the subject of a major crackdown by a reforming pope in Rome. As a penance, Losinga was ordered to build churches, something he did at Norwich, Yarmouth – and now Lynn. Losinga did what his tenants had asked him to, while making it clear the church was calling the shots. He authorised a weekly market, held each Saturday at the water's edge, and in 1101 built the Church of St Margaret of Antioch, to which a small priory was attached, on the marshy river bank. An annual fair was held in mid-June, the feast day of St Margaret. The history of Lynn had begun.

Rapid progress?

With the new church and the Saturday market as its focal point Lynn just grew and grew. Trade boomed, and with it the population. The course of the Great Ouse was altered, ensuring merchants could distribute the goods they imported with greater ease. Land was reclaimed from the sea, beginning around the Millfleet and Purfleet. It expanded inland and along the side of the river. Lynn was ideally placed. Apart from standing on the coast where it could benefit from the fishing industry and growing continental trade, it also stood at a transport crossroads. The three rivers in its vicinity flowed inland, and formed trade routes that were far better and easier to navigate than the poorly built roads of the day. To its west lay the Fens, at the time being opened up by sheep and cattle farmers. In time wool from the sheep would become England's greatest and most valuable export; the port of Lynn and much of East Anglia would become rich on the proceeds. The port also made profits from sale of agricultural goods grown on the fertile soil of the Fens. Later in the 1100s fresh development began to the north when a bridge was built across the Purfleet, in an area known as 'Newland'. This focused on St Nicholas's Chapel and a new market held on Tuesdays – which became today's Tuesday Market Place.

When did the 'King's' get put into Lynn?

For centuries, the town was known as Bishop's Lynn in honour of Bishop Herbert. In Losinga's Charter of 1101, addressed to his 'sons of Lynn', he granted St Margaret's to the jurisdiction of the monks of Norwich Cathedral. A century later King John granted the town another charter, giving it rights in trade and local government. The original church did not last long, sinking into the marshy ground. Renovation began again later in the 1100s, with enlargements and improvements at regular intervals over the next five centuries until it evolved into the massive building that exists today. The church boosted its revenues from tolls, rents, building licences and court fines, all of which increased along with trade. It was not until 1536, when the Reformation put paid to the monasteries in England, that King Henry VIII gained control. The town was henceforth known as 'King's Lynn'. Its people responded with an enduring royalism that lasted into the Civil War of the 1640s when it was the only place in Norfolk to rise – albeit only briefly and crushed after a short siege – against Parliament in favour of King Charles I.

Anything else?

In 2011 the Bishop of Norwich granted St Margaret's the honorary title of King's Lynn Minster. No doubt, more than a thousand years on, Herbert Losinga would have approved.

Daniel's Spanish journey

For a man of learning it must have been an illuminating moment. Norfolk cleric Daniel of Morley's trip to Muslim Spain in the late 12th century opened his eyes to a wider world – and helped people in his own country rediscover lost knowledge.

An intellectual odyssey?

Daniel of Morley was originally from the parish of Morley St Botolph, near Wymondham, in south Norfolk. He held the hereditary rectory of Flitcham, near Holkham, in the north of the county. Originally educated at the new university in Oxford, he must have been a man of means, for he managed to pay the large sum of 40 marks for land at Hillington in 1190. We also know he owed money to a Jewish moneylender at Castle Rising, and may have been a Royal Justice of the Peace at some stage of his life. His greatest achievement came during an extraordinary trip he took to Europe some time in the 1180s. At a time when few in western Europe had any kind of formal education or the means to travel, Daniel was seeking knowledge, and masters from overseas to teach him. He later wrote about this journey in glowing terms – but it got off to a bad start in Paris. There he found "nothing but ignoramuses expounding Roman law". The real intellectual heavyweights, he discovered, were to be found further to the south. In Spain – the city of Toledo, to be precise. So he "packed his bags and hurried there". To Daniel's satisfaction, in Toledo he attended lectures "from some of the wisest philosophers in the world". They included the Italian Gerardo de Cremona, a leading translator of scientific texts from Arabic into Latin who was to become a great influence on the Norfolk man.

A steep learning curve?

Daniel returned to England with a full head and "a pile of books". Initially he was disappointed to see English teachers rigidly teaching the same old thing. But his friendship with the Bishop of Norwich, John of Oxford, led to greater things. The bishop invited him to lecture on the wonderful things he'd learned from his Spanish journey. The result was a written work, Philosophia. This weighty tome was divided into two books, dealing with man, the creation of the world, the elements, nature of the stars and the usefulness of astrology. He was not the first to publish on these matters. Clerical writers such as Adelard of Bath were already cornering the market on natural sciences and mankind's place in the universe. But Daniel had the edge in that his sources included new translations of work on the natural sciences by Aristotle.

Why was this so special?

Aristotle's works were the holy grail in medieval learning. This 3rd century BC Greek polymath wrote on many different subjects, including physics, metaphysics, poetry, theatre, music, logic, rhetoric, politics, government, ethics, biology and zoology. His works had been largely lost in the west as a result of the chaos that followed the collapse of the Roman empire, but his name was still revered. It was the Arab scholars of Islam, as well as the Byzantine Greeks in Constantinople, who kept the light of learning alive in what became known subsequently as the Dark Ages. They protected as much of Aristotle's legacy as they could. The Arabs had been in Spain since they overran much of the country in the eighth century. Aristotle lay at the foundation of much of Islamic philosophy, inspiring many scholars. Even so, it is estimated only about a third of the ancient Greek's works survived. The Muslim kingdoms of Spain were celebrated for their learning in such subjects as mathematics and science. Toledo was famed for the relatively peaceful co-existence of Muslims, Christians and Jews – a rare thing. Ironically, while these major religions were fighting each other to the death during the crusades, some were trying to learn from one another. Was the Norfolk man aware of the contradictions?

Maybe he'd seen the light

He must have been a remarkable man. While most of his contemporaries were illiterate, and many of them held non-Christians such as Jews and Muslims in violent contempt, and many Muslims in turn denounced the Latin 'Franks' (as they called all from western Europe) as demons, Daniel was happy to learn from the 'enemy'. Scholars and teachers such as he kept the torch of learning lit for future generations. For him to get hold of original versions of Aristotle's On Generation and Corruption, Physics, On the Heavens and On Sense and Sensibilia was a real breakthrough. At this time there was no rigid division between arts and science – they were seen as one and the same subject, and remained so until relatively modern times. Of course, only a select audience was reading his words in copies laboriously hand-written and prohibitively expensive; his fellow clerics and monks largely, the university men of their day.

Not a mass publishing phenonomon then!

Eventually this kind of new learning led to a 'renaissance' of thought and education in the west, as well as a growing demand for the works of Aristotle. The knowledge was disseminated by later scholars. Daniel of Morley died in about 1210, by which time he was probably 60 years old. Robert Grosseteste, Bishop of Lincoln from 1235 until his death 18 years later, was born in Stradbroke, Suffolk. He was one who used the translations of Aristotle as a basis for scientific research, as did another clergyman, the Franciscan Adam Marsh. Best known was Roger Bacon. This Franciscan friar and Oxford scholar was born in 1214, four years after Daniel's death. Ahead of his time, he experimented in such fields as optics, mathematics and astrology. His inspiration and guides were the works of Aristotle and the Muslim academics. An all-round Renaissance man then, whose legacy lived long after his death in the work of his pupils and later admirers. This body of work eventually brought about the Enlightenment of the 17th and 18th centuries, when scientists such as Sir Isaac Newton flourished. But where would Roger Bacon have been without such pioneers as Daniel of Morley? His pile of books had helped create an unbroken line of learning. "If I have seen further," wrote Newton, "it is by standing on the shoulders of giants." The journey to Toledo had been worthwhile. The west had rediscovered its lost knowledge.

Anything else?

Bishop Grosseteste University sits close to Lincoln Cathedral. It specialises in teacher training.

You can read the biography of Daniel of Morley and other historical figures by logging on to the Oxford Dictionary of National Biography. It's free to use online via your local library, if you're a member.

13th century **1266**

The disinherited barons

"They loaded seven score carriages with plunder and murdered many of the citizens." The year was 1266, and Norwich was once again on the receiving end of some unruly and unwelcome visitors.

Who was it this time? Vikings or Normans?

The perpetrators of the sack of Norwich in December 1266, as recorded by the monks of the Bury Chronicle, were home-grown specimens. They were known as the 'Disinherited Barons', and they were subjecting much of East Anglia to their tender mercies from a base in the wild Fens. It would take all the skill and guile – and ferocity – of the future King Edward I to end their reign of terror.

Another civil war

The period from 1258 to 1267 saw parts of England racked by what is now called the Barons' War. King Henry III had upset his English nobles with high taxation and what they saw as his favouring of his French relatives. Only half a century earlier the barons had forced Henry's father, King John, to seal Magna Carta under duress, relinquishing some royal rights. In 1258 they were in the mood to do the same again. Roger Bigod, Earl of Norfolk, was among the nobles who rounded on the king at Oxford in that year and forced him to agree to their demands. It turned out to be the opening gambit in a decade of cat and mouse manoeuvres between royalists and rebels that ended in vicious warfare. When Henry III, like his father, reneged on the deal, the barons found their leader. He was Simon de Montfort, Earl of Leicester, known to history as the founder of England's first parliament. Although the formidable and ambitious de Montfort defeated the king and his son Prince Edward at Lewes in 1264, the royalists turned the tables the following year. At Evesham, amid great bloodshed, de Montfort was defeated and killed.

Peace at last. . .

The royalists were in vengeful mood. Henry confiscated the lands and property of the knights who had followed de Montfort. At a stroke they became landless outlaws – and acted accordingly. Civil wars were always bad news for ordinary people. They were caught in the middle between opposing armies, who were likely to assault, rob, threaten and generally make their lives miserable. When law and order broke down, anarchy reigned. John Deyville, one of Montfort's followers, gathered forces in the Isle of Ely. Safe on the island set in the undrained, trackless waterworld of the Fens, they could defy an army, much as Hereward the Wake did against the Normans in the 1070s and robber baron Geoffrey de Mandeville – "the devil in human form" – had done during the anarchy of the 1140s. Deyville's desperados were not quite in that league, but they had little to lose and caused mayhem throughout East Anglia while the royal army was busy elsewhere. Norwich was just one of the wealthy places they targeted; Cambridge and many smaller places felt the heat. Some rich people were abducted, to be ransomed at great expense by their families. The Bishop of Norwich, Roger of Scarning, was one of the citizens who fled to the sanctuary of Bury St Edmunds abbey.

Who was Deyville?

Sir John Deyville was a Nottinghamshire knight. Aged in his early thirties in 1266, he was one of the leading 'disinherited' rebels, having lost his lands in the midlands and Yorkshire. Like many of the rebels he was deeply in debt to Jewish moneylenders – and was quick to attack unpopular Jews, most notoriously at Lincoln. After initially holding out in the Isle of Axholme, Lincolnshire, he found a new base at Ely. Montfort's supporters were active elsewhere in the country, and the king feared invasion from France. Some of them, including Deyville, even seized the city of London before being expelled. Henry's siege of the Isle of Ely was a chaotic affair which was going nowhere. The king was no great warrior, and his amphibious assault was repulsed with heavy casualties. Enter his eldest son, Edward. Aged 28, he had matured into a feared and respected warrior who had already hounded Montfort to his death. Having been busy hunting rebels first in the north, then in London, it was not until the summer of 1267 that he arrived in the Fens. He had secured ships to bring troops in along the river route, cutting off the rebels' line of escape. By that time many of them were keen to surrender to the prince on favourable terms. Montfort's great bastion at Kenilworth in the Midlands had already given in. Its defenders secured terms – known as the Dictum of Kenilworth – that would allow them to buy their lands back by paying large fines to the crown. For men who defined themselves and their families by their ancestral lands, it was a price worth paying. Deyville duly surrendered to Prince Edward on July 1, 1267.

Everyone happy then?

John Deyville was formally pardoned, and paid a hefty £600 in instalments for the return of his lands. He died in 1290. Roger of Scarning returned safely to Norwich, but six years later he was involved in more trouble when the citizens and the monks fell out. It led to bloodshed on both sides and intervention by the king. Following a decade of civil war, the next few years were surprisingly peaceful in England. Fractious barons, who had rebelled against the crown several times in the past century, seemed content now they had their lands back; while townspeople and villagers were happy they finally had a strong and just king who would uphold the law and protect them and their property from the barons. England had endured a long period of unrest, and Norwich suffered with the rest; in 1173 its castle had been seized by Hugh Bigod, Earl of Norfolk, then in rebellion against Henry II, while in 1216 Prince Louis of France had seized the city in his bid to take the English crown. Weak government and incompetent kings had been to blame. Edward I, who succeeded his father as king in 1272, was one of the most efficient and powerful kings of medieval England – though for certain he has his critics in Wales and Scotland.

What happened in Norwich?

Having been sacked and looted by unwelcome visitors, the citizens had clearly had enough. Within 20 years of the 1266 raid they began work on the city walls, which were completed by 1343.

They shall not pass: A surviving fragment of the medieval city walls on Carrow Hill in Norwich.

14th century **1340**

A Yarmouth hero

When danger threatened England from the sea, East Anglians were often at the forefront in defence – and attack. Sir John Perebrown was one such. His finest hour came in 1340.

The Nelson touch?

Nobody could pretend the English navy of the 14th century was a patch on the later Royal Navy of Nelson, but in spirit it was not so far off. The coastal counties of Norfolk and Suffolk have produced innumerable sailors who gave good service to their country. At the outset of what became the Hundred Years War, France was poised to invade England, and Perebrown and his Norfolk crews were in the front line.

Wasn't the Hundred Years War fought in France?

Thanks to events at Sluys in 1340, it was. Three years earlier King Edward III revived the English claim to the throne of France that was to provoke war for the next century and a bit. He began mobilising troops and allies on the continent. The French were not going to take this lying down. Their king, Philip VI, prepared a pre-emptive strike that would take the war to England. French ships raided the southern coast at Southampton, Portsmouth, Folkestone, Dover, Hastings and Harwich, as well as the Channel Islands, while English troops made little headway on the continent. By 1340 the French king was ready to take the offensive. His fleet mustered off the coast of the Low Countries with the aim of landing in England. Sir John Perebrown (or Perebroune) was one of the foremost citizens of Great Yarmouth. A merchant, ship-owner and wine seller, he was MP for the borough of Yarmouth in the 1320s, bailiff of the town 15 times and helped collect money to build the town walls. Great Yarmouth had come a long way since it was a tiny spit of land rising from the sea in the 11th century. From a collection of seasonal fishing huts arose a mighty port, home to fishermen, intrepid merchants and fighting sailors. In 1208 King John granted the town a charter, making it a partially self-governing borough. Periods of boom and bust followed, but Yarmouth always looked out to sea. Its secure Yarmouth Roads granted shipping safe passage between the treacherous and deadly sand bars of the north Norfolk coast. In times of war, the kings of England turned to Yarmouth and other east coast ports for ships and men. Even the little port of Blakeney provided ships for the war, as did Cley and Wiveton (both of these medieval ports used to be important, but have now been left inland due to changes in our coastal landscape). Great Yarmouth was not to be outdone. In 1340 it provided 43 ships, and up to 1,000 men from the town and the surrounding area.

And Perebrown?

He enjoyed an interesting career. From his house in the Conge, he had become one of the wealthiest men in Great Yarmouth. It hadn't all been plain sailing. In 1314 in a dispute with the men of Southtown he had been forced to take refuge on one of his ships. A decade and a half later, however, he backed the young Prince Edward in his struggles following the death of his father, the ill-fated Edward II – a good career move, as the prince became the powerful King Edward III. By 1340 Perebrown was Admiral of the fleet north of the Thames, succeeding another Yarmouth man, Thomas de Drayton. Fighting at sea was far from the technical science it became in later years; in the medieval period naval battles were more like land battles on water, as ships had to come very close to one another before fighting began. Archers and men-at-arms were the deciding factor. Having said that, you needed competent sailors to navigate and manoeuvre successfully and gain an advantage, and in that the English were experts.

What happened at Sluys?

The French fleet was massed at an inlet by the town of Sluys (pronounced *Sloice*), between West Flanders and Zeeland in modern Holland. Edward sailed from the River Orwell in Suffolk with up to 250 ships. As well as East Anglia, the Kent ports made a great contribution. Late reinforcements from the north, led by Sir Robert Morley, also joined the king. The French fleet, part of which was made up of Genoese mercenaries aboard fast galleys, had numerical advantage. Most warships of the period were slow and cumbersome, little more than fighting platforms with small crews. They were known as cogs. King Edward was aboard the Cog Thomas. As he attacked, on the morning of June 24, the French were on the defensive, chained together in three or four lines, robbing them of their ability to manoeuvre. The English attacked in two lines, with the sun behind them, and outflanked their opponents. Edward's ships had considerable firepower, which proved decisive. Each ship was supported by two vessels with archers to shoot at men on the opposing ships – and we all know how good English archers were. Their longbowmen could shoot faster and at greater distance than their adversaries armed with crossbows. The men-at-arms then boarded, and it became savage hand-to-hand fighting. Combat must have been intense, as contemporaries reckoned it a particularly fierce battle, with the water said to be full of corpses and running red with blood. The French are reported to have lost 160 ships and up to 15,000 men, though all figures in medieval accounts have to be taken with a pinch of salt. At all events, it was a complete victory for England, with French admirals Quiéret and Béhuchet both killed. Some accounts say Edward was wounded by an arrow or crossbow bolt. His wife Queen Philippa was also present, and one of her ladies was reported killed in the battle.

What was the aftermath?

England gained control of the Channel. The threat of French invasion faded, as their fleet had been virtually destroyed. Edward was free to land troops on the continent. It was fortunate for the English people that invasion was avoided, for France was subsequently devastated by decades of warfare. This culminated in crushing English victories on land at Crecy and Poitiers. Norfolk continued to provide men and material. Seven years later Yarmouth sent ships to the successful siege of Calais, and they were matched by Blakeney's complement. In gratitude for Perebrown's efforts, Edward granted his home town the right to add three royal half-lions in its coat of arms in front of the existing tail ends of three herrings – a right exercised to this day.

Any heroic homecoming?

Sir John had little time in which to enjoy the fruits of victory. He died within three years. Sadly, his line died out when his son Farman died in 1349, probably a victim of the Black Death. It devastated the population of Yarmouth, but the town continued its proud naval tradition until modern times. Sir John is remembered in a modern Great Yarmouth street named after him.

15th century **1400**

The mystery plays

If you were in an East Anglian town on Whit Monday in the 1400s you were in for a feast of visual entertainment. Crowds gathered from near and far to see religious mystery – or miracle – plays.

Professional productions?

They were for local people by local people. Local tradespeople, to be precise – butchers, bakers, candlestickmakers and other allied trades gathered yearly in a collective effort that involved much of the population. By the 15th century, the height of the mystery plays' popularity, people travelled to cities like Norwich on holy days to watch them. There, the main centres of production were Tombland and Market Hill, where civic dignitaries would be seated to watch the entertainment.

Entertainment? In a religious age?

Miracle plays began as early as the 10th century. They were originally performed in churches by clerics to explain stories from the Bible and Christian calendar to a mainly illiterate flock who depended on visual aids for information. No doubt the clergymen doing the acting added spontaneously to the tales, and probably ad-libbed to keep the audience amused. Papal disapproval of clerics acting meant the clergy eventually handed over these plays to the laity. During the Middle Ages trade guilds were strong in Europe. Far more than just trades unions, they were a mixture of professional body, co-operative and beneficial society and religious organisation. The best known is the Guild of Saint George, England's patron saint. Formed in 1385, it eventually became the most powerful in Norwich. Other guilds were available, and all had their say. By the later Middle Ages they were creating lavish mystery plays. Some scholars maintain the word could derive from the Latin *misterium*, meaning craft, as in craft guilds. With elaborate costumes and stages built on movable wheeled vehicles which were often two storeys high, the pageants would move around the city performing in different places as they went.

Sounds like a full-time job

A document belonging to the Corporation of Norwich was discovered by a 19th century historian, Henry Harrod. Probably dating from the early 1400s, it casts detailed light on the city's mystery plays. By then the management and execution of the plays was in the hands of St Luke's Guild – the pewterers, braziers and bell-founders' union. Finding the cost exorbitant, they asked the Mayor to press the other trades to share the burden. The Mayor agreed, and other Norwich groups each took on a part of the play. The document breaks it down, and also gives us an insight into just what went on in a mystery play. They were known as the Corpus Christi (Body of Christ) cycle, and combined a number of individual tableaux. The first pageant displayed the Creation of the World, and was presented by the mercers, drapers and haberdashers. The glaziers, carpenters and wheelwrights landed everybody's favourite bit – the so-called Helle Carte. This was a depiction of the gates of hell, and gave people the chance to dress up as demons welcoming the damned, complete with dancing, costumed male and female devils accompanied by a satanic bagpiper.

Feeling a bit sorry for the damned...

People loved it – proper holiday entertainment for the thousands who watched it. We have no first-hand accounts of the Norwich plays, but contemporary accounts of similar events at places such as Chester indicate there was plenty of earthy humour. Moving on, the grocers and chandlers did Adam and Eve; the fullers, woollen weavers and masons got Cain and Abel; Noah's Ark (Noyse Shipp) was handled by the bakers, brewers, innkeepers and cooks; the story of Moses and the Exodus was the responsibility of the tanners and cordwainers; the smiths hammered out David and Goliath, while the dyers, braziers, pewterers and goldsmiths performed the Birth of Christ, complete with Shepherds and the Three Kings; Christ's baptism was taken on by the barbers, surgeons, hatters, skinners, pursers and bagmakers, plus assorted trades; the butchers, fishmongers and watermen gave their take on the Resurrection, while the worsted weavers completed the bill with Judgment Day.

A cast of hundreds!

No doubt it was a family affair, and it was probably highly competitive with each group trying to outdo the other. Costumes could take weeks to prepare.

For example, angels' wings were made out of goose feathers. The pageant vehicles would have colourful painted scenery – it is little wonder the Guild of Saint Luke needed some help. Musicians would have accompanied the singing that went with the plays. The original Latin text had to be replaced by English in order for people to understand what was happening. Rather like modern pantomime, it is likely topical references would be thrown in that audiences would easily understand. (Oh yes, they were!) In the Chester version elements of domestic humour were a feature of the Noah's Ark pageant, centred on Noah and his wife bickering. There may also have been an element of advertising; if your guild did a good job, it can't have been bad for business.

Sounds great. Why did it have to end?

Mystery plays and other holiday pageants were thriving in the early 1500s. In Norwich plays such as Saint George and the Dragon were popular until the 1530s. The Reformation changed everything. The new Church of England suppressed the guilds, and the plays died out. Henry Harrod, writing 400 years later, recorded that the Grocers' Company broke up in the 1540s and sold a dilapidated carriage, the last of their pageant vehicles – no doubt with heavy hearts. The fun wasn't over though; the city fathers, in their new form as the Company of Saint George, ditched the saint, but kept the dragon. Anyone who has read Thomas Hardy's Return of the Native will recall that the tale of Saint George and the Dragon was being played out well into the 19th century. 'Snap', the representation of a dragon, has survived to this day, and can be seen at the Castle Museum and Art Gallery. Norwich being an old-fashioned kind of a place, an echo of the pomp and pageantry survived, with trades marching to the cathedral preceded by banners. This ended when the old Corporation was abolished by a modernising liberal government in 1835. During the early 21st century mystery plays were revived at places such as York and Chester, an echo of the community involvement of the Middle Ages. 'Snap' performs each July in the Norwich Lord Mayor's Procession, a modern echo of the pageantry of the Middle Ages.

Anything else?

The trade guilds could also get involved in local politics. Politics being a funny old business, this could sometimes end in tears, as we will soon see in the sad story of Gladman's Rising.

15th century **1415**

Erpingham's strike

Good morrow, old Sir Thomas Erpingham!
A good soft pillow for that good white head
Were better than a churlish turf of France

Not so, my liege - this lodging likes me better.
Since I may say, 'Now lie I like a king'.

This exchange is between Shakespeare's King Henry V and his earl marshal on the eve of the Battle of Agincourt, in 1415. It introduces us to the man in command of the most lethal arm of war produced in the Middle Ages – the English and Welsh longbowmen. Sir Thomas Erpingham, as Shakespeare indicates, was a veteran in his fifties. It is little wonder the young king relied upon him and trusted him, for his support was rock solid. This Norfolk-born soldier had been a loyal servant to Henry's father and grandfather before him. Sir Thomas Erpingham has only a walk-on part in Shakespeare's most famous history play, but his career was far more interesting than that.

Any connection to a village in north Norfolk?

Thomas was born at Erpingham, four miles from Aylsham, in about 1355 or 1357 to a family with a claim to have been settled there since the time of William the Conqueror. He was later granted lands near King's Lynn. By some accounts his military career began as a teenager, serving under Edward the Black Prince (son of King Edward III) in southern France. England was still fighting the Hundred Years War, and the military campaigns there have entered history for their brutality and bloodthirstiness; it would have been a 'baptism of fire' which surely taught the difference between chivalry and real warfare. Little is recorded of Thomas's early life until, at the age of 22, he appears as an esquire in the retinue of John of Gaunt, the Duke of Lancaster. Another of Edward III's many sons, Gaunt owned land in Norfolk and is particularly associated with Aylsham, so it was logical for Thomas to seek service with him. It was the beginning of a lifelong association with the

Lancastrian branch of the royal family that would lead him to stand at Henry V's side in France in 1415.

He was a professional soldier?

He came from the military caste, so it was expected of him. Not that he was any old mercenary or common soldier. The first mention of a soldiering role comes in 1381, when he was one of the commissioners charged with putting down the Peasants' Revolt in Norfolk. At the same time as Wat Tyler and the men of Kent and Essex were threatening London, trouble broke out in East Anglia. Geoffrey Lister, from Felthorpe, led a rising that briefly seized Norwich, but was crushed after a battle near North Walsham. Following that Thomas joined John of Gaunt on a Spanish campaign, and fought with the Teutonic knights in Lithuania and what became Prussia. The knights were a crusading order intent on converting pagans in eastern Europe to Christianity – by whatever means necessary. They receive an honourable mention in Chaucer's Canterbury Tales; indeed, Erpingham's career could gave been modelled on that of the dashing Knight in the Tales. In 1392 he also accompanied Gaunt to Jerusalem, by which time he had been knighted by him. Following Gaunt's death, he became a stalwart follower of his son Henry Bolingbroke, who was to become King Henry IV.

Anything to do with the Wars of the Roses?

That came about 50 years later, but the seeds of that complicated conflict were sown at this time. The problems arose with the competing claims of Edward III's children. During the 1390s Bolingbroke fell out with his cousin, now King Richard II. Sent into exile, he was accompanied by the loyal Erpingham, who was with him when he landed with forces at Ravenspur in 1399. In an effective coup d'etat, it was Erpingham who ambushed and captured Richard in Wales. The king was imprisoned in the Tower of London. He resigned the throne, and was murdered the following year. This new Lancastrian dynasty led by Henry IV was very insecure in its early years; there were constant rebellions and plots, culminating in the Battle of Shrewsbury against the powerful northern Percy clan (Shakespeare's Harry Hotspur). This is the first time young Prince Hal – later Henry V – enters the tale. As a 16-year-old, the then Prince of Wales was in the thick of it at Shrewsbury, and survived an arrow wound to the head. It is tempting to imagine the experienced Erpingham acting as his mentor. As Earl Marshal of England, he was the most important soldier in the kingdom. Made Constable of Dover Castle and Warden of the Cinque Ports, he was on the front line of southern England's defences against France. By 1401 he was a Knight of the Garter and served as ambassador to the French court, but he had not forgotten his Norfolk roots. He helped Norwich get a new charter from the king, enabling the citizens to elect a mayor and sheriffs.

On to Agincourt. . .

The new King Henry V revived his claim to the French crown, and invaded in 1415. Erpingham played a leading part. After besieging and capturing the port of Harfleur the English army, depleted by sickness, found itself on the banks of the River Somme threatened by a reinvigorated French force out for revenge. Henry was outnumbered by about six to one but he had one deadly and feared weapon; his archers. Hated by the French, these tough men from the shires of England and Wales had been trained from a young age to draw huge war bows, and fire them with instinctive accuracy. The French had already been defeated with horrible loss of life at battles 50 years earlier – at Crecy and Poitiers – so they should have learned the lesson. This time they hoped crossbowmen they had hired from the Italian state of Genoa would be their secret weapon. But the October rain affected the complicated machinery of the otherwise effective crossbowmen, and turned the turf into a muddy boobytrap. French numbers were negated as they found themselves trapped in a narrow battlefield. Sir Thomas Erpingham led the archers. On his command – *'Nestroque!'* ('Now strike!' probably delivered in Norfolk dialect) the longbow cut the chivalry of France to ribbons. They lost some 9,000 dead to just 150 to 300 English casualties.

And back home to Norfolk

The wars over (for now) the victors reaped the rewards. Erpingham had married twice, to Joan Clopton in about 1404 and Joan Walton in 1413, but had no children. It was time to secure his legacy. He began the building of St Mary's Church in his home village of Erpingham, and also helped fund Norwich Cathedral with the building of the Erpingham Gate. His statue stands there still, kneeling in the centre of a tall flint-faced gable, and visitors pass under it every time they go to the cathedral. On his death in 1428, aged 73, Erpingham was buried there. In October, 2015 the village of Erpingham held events to honour his role on the 600th anniversary of Agincourt.

15th century **1443**

Gladman's Rising

A mixture of city hall politics, carnival capers and town and gown rivalry led to the medieval shenanigans known as Gladman's Insurrection.

A mob of revolting peasants?

Far from it. The unrest which gripped Norwich in January, 1443, was a city affair. Its leading exponents, and most of the actors, were wealthy merchants and officials of the growing city. When a dispute over water mills, city boundaries and local politics got out of hand it ended up with the king intervening – and plenty of people in hot water. John Gladman was a city merchant and a member of one of the city's trade guilds. Guilds were vital to the life of pre-Reformation England. Membership gave individuals certain standing and privileges. The most important guild was that of Saint George. It honoured the saint's feast day (April 23) and gave help to members in need. Many of the city's influential merchants and officials were in the guild, and joined the ritual processions that marked holy days. These elaborate occasions featured elements of dressing up and the temporary suspension of social order and hierarchy. That of Saint George included a mock battle between the legendary saint and the figure of the dragon – 'Snap' – a man dressed in the colourful costume of a dragon with snapping jaws who went among the crowds in order to terrify onlookers. All good fun, but it had a serious side. We do not know if Gladman was a member of the Saint George guild, but he was accustomed to parade through the streets on Shrove Tuesday dressed as a king. This would be central to the events of 1443.

What had this got to do with city politics?

Since 1404, thanks to the charter granted by King Henry IV, Norwich had been given the status of a county, and had become self-governing. A total of 60 members were elected by the city freemen – a small fraction of the male population – to the assembly. A mayor was chosen annually, and two sheriffs. The charter had, though, left the city's boundaries undetermined. In the past this had led to clashes with surrounding hamlets and religious houses, in particular Carrow Priory and the monks of the cathedral. In 1272 there had been bloodshed between city and priory, and Norwich had been hit with a massive fine by the king. The city's enhanced status opened a new chapter in this occasionally acrimonious relationship. It was made worse by the political and personal machinations within the assembly. It was split between supporters of former mayor Thomas Wetherby – "of greate goods and greate pride" – and those of current mayor William Hempstede. Wetherby had been accused of rigging an election in the 1430s. Fined £100 and stripped of office, there remained a legacy of bitterness. He took revenge by making common cause with the Abbot of Saint Benet's monastery to embarrass the city authorities. Water mills had recently been built on the River Wensum (still called New Mills) but the abbot claimed they were obstructing the river, to which he held some rights. The Earl of Suffolk found in favour of the abbot and ordered the city to pull down the mills. Unrest began to fester. On January 25, 1443, the city assembly was in uproar about whether the city should use its seal to ratify an indenture of arbitration in the ongoing dispute. At the centre of the argument was a legal document in the possession of the cathedral prior which the citizens felt should be returned to them. Before long John Gladman was marching at the head of a procession reckoned by some accounts as 3,000 strong. (An exaggeration; the population was less than 10,000, so it was more likely in the hundreds). Gladman rode through the streets in mocking impersonation of a king, wearing a paper crown with attendants bearing a sceptre and sword. The crowd arrived at the priory gates, demanding the return of the documents, by some accounts calling out: "Let us burn the priory and kill the prior and monks." Although the priory was barely involved in the dispute, it was a target for popular discontent. The terrified monks handed over the document, and the threat was lifted.

They couldn't get away with it!

The arrival of the Duke of Norfolk and Earl of Oxford, although armed with a royal commission, resulted in more defiance by the citizens. The rioters held the city for a week before backing down and throwing themselves on the king's mercy. Nobody had been killed, and there was a ritual element to the riot that suggested the instigators expected a measured response. As it was, nobody was hanged. But the mayor was imprisoned, the city handed another big fine of 1,000 marks, and its government suspended by the king for the next four years.

15th century **1471**

The butcher's boy

He was the Suffolk boy prodigy who grew up to run the country. The workaholic who rose from humble roots to high office, the 'go-to' man the king relied upon for 20 years. He was a religious moderate, a humane man in a tough age, and an educationist with a sensitive touch way ahead of his time. So why has Thomas Wolsey received such a mixed press?

Hmmm. . . a little matter of greed, pride and corruption?

Or perhaps, he was just in the wrong place at the wrong time. More of that later. Young Thomas first saw the light of day in Ipswich in about 1471. He was born in his father's tavern close to St Mary Elms Church, near the spot where the Black Horse pub now stands. Cottages on the north side of the churchyard are the oldest inhabited in the town, and the view of the church would have been familiar to his parents. They moved to a house in St Nicholas Street when Thomas was a toddler. There is controversy over his father's occupation and character. He was a butcher, sometimes described as a grazier. According to the late Dr John Blatchly, local historian and former Ipswich School headmaster, Wolsey senior was a bit of a rough diamond. "He was a roughneck," he told me back in 2010. "He was often up before magistrates for selling bad meat pies, dumping offal into the street and allowing his swine to wander free, unattended. Thomas had a rough father, but a rather more couth mother." Mother Joan was sister to Edmund Daundy, bailiff, MP and leading magistrate of Ipswich. It was this uncle who paid for Thomas's education, first at the town's grammar school, then at Magdalen College, Oxford.

What was so special about Thomas Wolsey?

His earliest biographer, George Cavendish, wrote: "Being but a child, he was very apt at learning; by means whereof his parents, or his good friends and masters, conveyed him to the University of Oxford, where he progressed so in learning that, as he told me in his own person, he was called the boy-bachelor, forasmuch as he was made Bachelor of Arts at fifteen years of age." Later he became master at Magdalen, giving him an experience of teaching he was later to pass on to his home town. But his destiny lay outside Suffolk. Clerics in those days were civil servants, the best educated people in the country. By the early 1500s he had a government position in London. When the teenage Henry VIII came to the throne in 1509 he needed someone to take on the hard grind of government work, while the young monarch concentrated on jousting, hunting and other pleasurable activities needed to forge a reputation as the Renaissance's most glamorous prince.

He needed Wolsey. . .

"Wolsey was immensely able, a workaholic," according to John Blatchly. For the next 20 years he took on job after job, becoming Henry's Chancellor. He organised war and peace, economic policy, law and the Church at home and foreign policy overseas. Government was still small enough for one man to – just about – cover all bases. He made enemies, as all politicians do. Many resented his wealth, and the way he flaunted it. The old aristocracy could never forgive the 'new men' raised by the Tudor regime for supplanting their authority and influence over the king. As the 1520s dawned, however, Wolsey enjoyed his finest hour. Henry VIII's greatest desire was to cut a dash on the European stage. He invaded France. Wolsey organised cash, troops, ships, and when it resulted in an expensive stalemate he made sure Henry still looked good. In 1520 he and the French King Francis came together at peace talks organised by Wolsey. It is remembered today for the wealth displayed at the scene, christened the 'Field of the Cloth of Gold' for all the bling on show.

What was happening at home?

War cost money. Taxes rose, and discontent grew. In places such as Lavenham in Suffolk workers in the vital woollen trade were angry at high taxation. Riots broke out, and many blamed Wolsey as the king's chief minister. While he had Henry's favour he remained unassailable. As he got older he wished to pass on the gift of learning that had made his own career. He founded a school in Ipswich. In 1528 he created the Cardinal College of St Mary in Ipswich, linked to his old Oxford college, hoping it would rival the likes of Eton. He had not visited his home town for years. Perhaps unwilling to leave the capricious king to his own devices for too long, he stayed close to the court, but he had not forgotten his roots. He published his own book, on the rudiments of grammar, designed to be used in every English school. Wolsey sought to make learning enjoyable. Not for him the 'spare the rod, spoil the child' philosophy. "Pleasure is to mingle with study, that the child may think learning rather an amusement than a toil," he told his teachers. "Tender youth is to suffer neither severe thrashings nor sour, threatening looks."

That'll never catch on. How was King Henry behaving himself?
It all went hideously wrong for Wolsey at the end of the 1520s. When Henry wanted to divorce his wife, Katharine of Aragon, and marry Anne Boleyn, Wolsey was caught in the crossfire. By now he was Cardinal Wolsey, a papal legate, as well as Archbishop of York and Lincoln. This very grandeur, once an asset, helped to doom him. Things went badly with the pope, who would not grant a divorce. Now Wolsey was vulnerable. The 'butcher's boy' had failed, and his enemies circled. His greed, pride and alleged corruption were used against him. Henry turned nasty. In vain, the Cardinal tried to placate the king, granting him his great palace at Hampton Court to deflect his anger. Too late. Wolsey died at Leicester in November, 1530, already stripped of office, under arrest and halfway to London charged – unjustly – with treason.

What happened next?
Wolsey's death and disgrace doomed his Ipswich school. Three things remain; Wolsey's Gate, a riverside entrance, St Peter's Church and the foundation stone. His posthumous reputation also suffered. As England turned towards Protestantism Wolsey was a symbol of the ousted Catholic church.
Shakespeare later imagined a conversation between him and his successor Thomas Cromwell:
O Cromwell, Cromwell! Had I but served my God with half the zeal
I served my king, He would not in mine age
Have left me naked to mine enemies.
In recent times Wolsey's star has been rising. Unlike Sir Thomas More, with whom he has been unfavourably compared, he did not burn heretics. Wolsey was inclined to show mercy to dissenters believing, like Queen Elizabeth I, that the state should not "make windows into men's souls". Perhaps the history of the Reformation would have been less savage had Wolsey's moderate, slightly cynical, toleration prevailed.

In 2011 a statue of Thomas Wolsey was unveiled in Ipswich, at the junction of Silent Street and St Peter's Street, near to his birthplace. Dr Blatchly, who died in 2015, was chairman of the Thomas Cardinal Wolsey Project.

15th century **1485**

Jockey of Norfolk

'Jockey of Norfolk, be not too bold, for Dickon thy master is bought and sold. . .'

Sounds ominous. . .

This warning, supposedly issued before the Battle of Bosworth in August, 1485, proved all too accurate. For both King Richard III and John 'Jockey' Howard, first Duke of Norfolk, the day was to prove lethal. Both men died fighting in one of the most decisive and influential battles ever fought on English soil.

Lancastrian or Yorkist?

Both Richard and John Howard were of the White Rose fraternity. Richard was a member of the House of York, while Howard helped to secure East Anglia for the Yorkists. They went back a long way, and were related through the customary aristocratic marriages. The Howard family had risen from relatively obscure origins during the 15th century. Their roots were at Wiggenhall, in Norfolk, where John's grandparents lived. Close association with the Mowbrays, the family which held the title of the Dukes of Norfolk in the 1400s, boosted their prestige. First and foremost, the Howards were a fighting clan. It was by military service to the crown that they rose to the pinnacle of society. John, a man of "average height with a strong, square face" was known familiarly as Jack, or Jock – hence the nickname 'Jockey'. Born in 1421, he fought alongside the Yorkists at such battles as Towton in 1461. There, the teenage Edward of York avenged his father's death in a decisive and extremely bloody victory over the Lancastrians in Yorkshire, and was able to seize the crown as a result. Impressed by his steadfast performance, Edward IV (who was Richard's elder brother) promoted Howard to Constable of Norwich Castle, Sheriff of Norfolk and Suffolk and Treasurer of the Royal Household. In 1470 he was elevated to the peerage as Lord Howard. By now at the veteran stage of his career, he successfully commanded an English fleet against the Scots in 1481-2, aided by his eldest son, Thomas.

All very straightforward – and Edward IV looked set for a long reign. . .
For Yorkist loyalists such as the Howards, a crisis came in 1483 when the king suddenly and unexpectedly died. In one of the most controversial episodes in English history, Richard, then Duke of Gloucester, took the crown after Edward's two sons were declared illegitimate. Debate has raged for many years about Richard's motives, and whether he had the 'Princes in the Tower' murdered. The water has been so muddied by later Tudor propaganda and Shakespearian dramatics which destroyed Richard's reputation that the truth is hard to come by. What is certain is that in the 1483 coup the Howards backed Richard, their old friend and ally. For their support John became the new Duke of Norfolk (the Mowbray line had recently died out) while son Thomas became Earl of Surrey. The dukedom was one of the most important in the peerage of the realm; it carried with it the hereditary posts of Earl Marshal and Admiral of England. These were no empty sinecures, but responsible roles that meant the Duke of Norfolk was the chief soldier in the land. He was the 'go-to' man when enemies from France or Scotland threatened. Norfolk was subsequently referred to as the 'first' duke, as the title was considered a new creation.

The king's right hand man?
For the two years of Richard's troubled reign, Norfolk was his most loyal subject. He helped him defeat a rebellion by the Duke of Buckingham and, when Henry Tudor invaded from the west in the summer of 1485, Richard knew he could rely on 'Jockey' to bring forces from the east. He could rely on few others though. Other 'allies', such as the Duke of Northumberland and the Stanley family, Earls of Derby, were less reliable. On August 22, battle loomed – and the two armies went head to head at Bosworth Field in Leicestershire. In theory, Richard had the upper hand, with 10,000 troops against Henry's 7,000. But a large proportion of Richard's army fought under the Stanley banner, and their loyalty was in question. On the night of the battle, according to legend, Norfolk found a note attached to his tent; "Jockey of Norfolk be not too bold, for Dickon thy master is bought and sold". Perhaps he laughed it off as enemy propaganda, or perhaps he saw his own doom. Whatever his reaction, the 64-year-old duke prepared for battle.

A horse, a horse, my kingdom for a horse. . .
Richard divided his forces into three divisions, or 'battles'. In the spearhead

was the Duke of Norfolk, along with his son as his second-in-command. Norfolk attacked Lancastrian troops under the Earl of Oxford, but made little headway, and some of his men ran away. In the melee his helmet's face guard was torn away. A Lancastrian arrow hit him in the face, and he fell dead. Stung by Norfolk's death Richard called for reinforcements, but the Duke of Northumberland failed to respond. The king led a headlong charge at the Lancastrians, hoping to kill Henry Tudor. At that point the Stanleys intervened – on Henry's side. It was the decisive moment. Richard's fate was sealed. Although he got close enough to Henry to kill his standard bearer, he was surrounded by Tudor's spearmen. He could have escaped on horseback, but chose to fight to his tragic, bloody end. According to Shakespearian legend, his crown was found in a bush and handed to Henry on the battlefield. As we now know, Richard's body was buried in nearby Leicester, and created a huge stir when it was discovered there underneath a car park in 2012. The king, last of the Plantagenet line, was reburied at Leicester's cathedral amid great pomp and pageantry three years later. The nearby King Richard III Visitor Centre is now a popular tourist attraction.

What happened next?

Henry VII founded the Tudor dynasty. He sneekily dated his reign to the day before the battle, thus making all those who fought for Richard – their lawful king at the time – traitors. Norfolk's son Thomas survived the battle, and was imprisoned and lost land and titles. But the Tudors needed good fighters, and he was partially redeemed when appointed Lieutenant General of the North, protecting the border from the Scots. His full rehabilitation had to wait until 1513 when he and his son led an English army to a stunning victory over the invading Scots at Flodden in Northumberland. For this great service the family's full titles and lands were restored. John Howard's grandson, the third duke, was a major player in the reign of Henry VIII. Two of his nieces – Anne Boleyn and Catherine Howard – married the king, with tragic results. The title of Duke of Norfolk has remained in the family to this day.

16th century **1531**

Burning issues of faith

On Norwich's Riverside Road stands a plaque. It records a place used for public executions in the Tudor period. One of its prominent victims was a man burnt at the stake in the summer of 1531, called by some historians the 'Father of the English Reformation'. He was Thomas Bilney.

An unfamiliar name

A shadowy character, he is little known today. But the list of people he influenced reads like a roll-call of early English Protestantism; Hugh Latimer and Matthew Parker, future Archbishop of Canterbury, among their number. Thomas Bilney was an unlikely martyr. Born in 1495, either in Norwich or the village of East Bilney, near Dereham, we know little of his early life. Short of stature, but tall in conviction, this shy scholar attended Trinity Hall, Cambridge, with the view of becoming a priest. So far, so orthodox – but his life was changed by reading the works of an influential continental thinker. Dutchman Desiderius Erasmus published his New Testament in Greek in 1516. His way of thinking has become known as Humanism. Based on close study of the Scriptures, it emphasised an intellectual approach to God. For those who were becoming disillusioned with what they saw as the abuses and old-fashioned superstition of the Catholic Church, it was a revelation. "Immediately, I felt a marvellous comfort and quietness," Bilney wrote of reading Erasmus. Although he took holy orders in 1519 he was on a collision course with the authorities. It is likely he also read the works of German reformer Martin Luther, whose publication of his '95 theses' in 1517 was about to plunge Europe into religious conflict.

What did he have against the Church?

Like most contemporary reformers he wanted to see an end to such 'corrupt' practices as the sale of indulgences, veneration of saints' relics and the pilgrimages that went along with them. But Bilney did not question the authority of the pope or the Church's accepted wisdom on the controversial issue of transubstantiation, the miraculous conversion of bread and wine into the body and blood of Christ at consecration. He was to remain orthodox on these subjects for the rest of his short life. In 1525 he was licensed to preach throughout the diocese of Ely, and began putting forward his reformist views as an itinerant preacher throughout Norfolk and Suffolk. He began to attract supporters; Matthew Parker, the Norwich man who would become archbishop under Elizabeth I many years later, and the Cambridge academic Hugh Latimer. This former conservative was won over by Bilney, saying after listening to his friend "by his confession I learned more than in 20 years before". Latimer was himself burnt as a heretic under Queen Mary in 1555.

Worth dying for: This plaque in Norwich marks the place where Thomas Bilney was put to death in 1531.

So much for supporters. Any critics?

Plenty. Initially Cardinal Wolsey, in charge of Church policy, was inclined to tolerate the reformers, so long as they did not challenge his authority outright. But these were dangerous times. In Germany the religious ferment ignited by Luther had led to a devastating peasants' rebellion which threatened the social order. People in England were alarmed. Already there were calls from reformers for a Bible in English; religious conservatives were clamping down on this. Wolsey summoned Bilney and made him promise not to teach Luther's incendiary doctrines. But in 1527 he preached sermons in and near London denouncing idolatry – and was soon in trouble. He was arrested and imprisoned in the Tower. Arraigned before Wolsey, Warham, Archbishop of Canterbury, and several bishops in the chapter-house at Westminster, he was convicted of heresy. Under heavy pressure he agreed to recant – deny his earlier views.

So he was spared?

After a year in the Tower Bilney was freed. For all the bloodthirsty reputation of the times, if heretics admitted they were in the wrong they were usually spared. But, in an age of conscience, many who did so when threatened with death later regretted their decision. So it was with Bilney. On returning to Cambridge he wrestled with his sense of guilt, and eventually resumed preaching. Unable to speak in churches he spoke in open fields to the poor, and harangued church congregations as they left services. By now he was a marked man. On a visit to Norwich he gave a copy of William Tyndale's English translation of the New Testament to Katherine Manne, an anchoress (religious hermit) at Norwich's Dominican friary. This was a dangerous move; publishing the Bible in anything but Latin was an offence. Tyndale himself was in hiding in the Netherlands (where he was eventually executed by strangling). Bishop of Norwich Richard Nix arrested Bilney, and he was found guilty of heresy.

No chance of a reprieve this time?

In London, by 1531 Sir Thomas More was the new Chancellor. Later martyred for his principles, and canonised by the Catholic Church in the 20th century, he is best known today as the 'Man for all Seasons' of Robert Bolt's play. Despite his saintly reputation he was an iron-hard conservative who hated heresy. When More was asked to provide legal permission for Bilney's execution he did not hesitate, saying the proper course would have been to "burn him first and procure a writ afterwards". The night before his execution Bilney was held in the Norwich Guildhall, then used as a prison. Friends made one last attempt to get him to recant. To demonstrate his determination he thrust his hand into a candle flame, allowing the flame to consume one of his fingers. On August 19, 1531, Bilney was led along Bishopgate over the bridge to the area known as 'Lollards Pit' where earlier heretics had died. "Good people, I am come hither to die," he told the crowd before being burnt. He died mercifully quickly. Today the Lollards Pit pub (formerly Bridge House) near the site marks the spot.

And his influence on the Reformation?

East Anglia was to become a hotbed of Protestantism during the Reformation. The example set by a few brave people, such as Bilney, showed that reform was in the air. Within ten years Bibles in English were in every church, and religious disputes would divide the country for generations. Something which would no doubt have saddened Thomas Bilney, a man who wanted freedom of thought and expression.

16th century **1538**

A break with the past

Monasteries, abbeys and nunneries were part of the landscape and life of medieval East Anglia. After standing for centuries, they were left to rot within a few years in the mid-16th century. Only their eerie ruins remain.

What did the monasteries ever do for us?

Well. . . alms for the poor, education in an age when there was none on offer for the common people elsewhere, free hospitality to pilgrims, spreading religion throughout the country, stunning architecture and riches. . . that said, the monasteries were often controversial. In cities and towns like Norwich and Bury St Edmunds their privileges and rights were the targets of popular discontent. They were, many citizens felt, a bit too big for their boots. Abbeys and monasteries had begun life in Anglo-Saxon times. Often they were constructed in lonely spots where brethren could get back to basics; places like the then inaccessible fens where religious houses at places like Ramsey, Ely, Thorney and Crowland sprang up. In the marshy Broads the monastery of Saint Benet at Holme traced its origins to the pre-Conquest era. Following the Norman conquest the Benedictine order founded institutions at more populated spots, including Norwich Cathedral. The Cluniacs moved in at Castle Acre and Thetford, becoming renowned for colourful and ornate decoration. Orders of austere friars, themselves formed as a reaction against supposed corruption in these earlier monasteries, rejected possessions and moved in to places such as Norwich during the 1200s; the city eventually had four separate friaries. Perhaps the grandest abbey of the lot was that at Bury Saint Edmunds, which traced its roots back to the martyred King Edmund in the ninth century. It was powerful and wealthy.

A bit too wealthy perhaps?

These self-contained communities had land and power over their neighbours, which many people resented. The abbot of Bury, in particular, acted like a great magnate, dispensing justice and levying rents. They also had many servants and 'lay brothers' whose supposedly luxurious lives made them unpopular. As townspeople grew more assertive, the monasteries seemed to dig their heels in. In Norwich there were anti-priory riots in 1272 and 1443, Bury was almost destroyed in 1327, while in the Peasants' Revolt of 1381 major and minor religious houses were attacked. Institutions such as Binham, in north Norfolk and the nunnery at Carrow, Norwich, were forced to hand over land ownership documents to rebels. The prior of Bury was beheaded during the uprising.

Were they really unpopular?

These incidents would imply that, but the monasteries also attracted great devotion. People arranged to be buried in them, left money in their wills and had strong family links. They probably had mixed feelings about the institutions. By the early 1500s, reform was in the air. Checks on monastic corruption revealed several scandals. Whether monastic life was in decline or not, the crucial instigator of change was King Henry VIII. In the early 1530s his marital difficulties caused turmoil. Breaking with the Roman Catholic Church, he was declared Supreme Head of the English Church. This was a radical step, leaving England isolated in a largely Catholic Europe. Historian David Starkey recently characterised this as "Henry VIII's Hard Brexit". Parliament authorised the king to take control of monasteries. This was revolution from above. A nationwide programme of 'visitations' was organised by reform-minded Secretary of State Thomas Cromwell. When commissioners arrived at religious houses, they were looking for examples of monastic corruption and 'laxity' – and were rarely disappointed. In 1536 the first of the smaller, less influential houses, places such as Bromholm in Norfolk, surrendered to the king, and were dissolved.

Was there no opposition?

In Lincolnshire and the north people rose up to defend the monasteries and traditional religion. This 'Pilgrimage of Grace' gained widespread support and seriously rattled Henry, but after initially agreeing to the rebels' demands and getting them to stand down, he took terrible revenge with a wave of executions. The abbots of Colchester and Glastonbury were hanged, drawn and quartered. Unrest threatened to spread to Norfolk, but the king's savage reaction proved a powerful disincentive. Which of us would have the courage to defy the Tudor monarch in that kind of mood? Most priors and monks made a pragmatic deal; surrender and receive a pension, maybe even a nice, secure job with the new regime. Thus William Rugge, Saint Benet's abbot, became the new Bishop of Norwich. 1538 was the major year for dissolution there; the cathedral priory, Carrow Priory, and all four city friaries went, along with Wymondham Abbey. Castle Acre had surrendered the previous November. In 1539 they were joined by Binham, Peterborough, Bury, Ramsey, Thorney and Crowland. Thetford went the next year. The king's men seized everything valuable, including saints' relics once prized by pilgrims. Metals, including church bells, were melted down to be used as cannons for Henry's army in wars against the French.

Who won – and who lost?

Local gentry and aristocracy, plus town elites, did rather nicely, thank you very much. The Duke of Norfolk now owned the sites of three of the four Norwich friaries, as well as that of Castle Acre; the Paston family got hold of Binham and Norwich's Augustinian friary, in King Street; the Cromwell family asset-stripped Ramsey so thoroughly that only a gatehouse remained. However, Norwich's Dominican friary, Blackfriars, was bought by the city corporation, and still enjoys a useful life. (For one thing, it hosts the city's annual Beer Festival.) Most other sites were left to decay once useful material had been cannibalised; Bury went that way, and its ruins still stand ghost-like in the centre of the town. Norwich priory, Ely and Peterborough did better; they became cathedrals, so survived – gloriously. Many monks had little to complain about; the pensions offered by the government were generous enough to live on and, if they did not do as well as abbots and priors, at least they got something. Losers included the abbey servants. They were evicted to join the ranks of the desperately poor. Now there was no more charity given by the religious houses, who was going to look after them? Norwich, in particular, had many paupers, their numbers increasing as the textile trade was in a period of decline. Harsh 'Poor Laws' were enacted as law and order was threatened. A bad time to be poor.

Any stubborn, hard core diehards?

At isolated little Denny Abbey, near Ely, one stood out. Dame Elizabeth Throckmorton, head of an order of Poor Clares, had been ordered out in 1536. But it took three years to evict her and her 25 nuns. Even then she retired to a private house and continued to live according to her order's strict rule until her death eight years later.

A Queen's resting place

In 1536 an English queen was buried at Peterborough Cathedral. Katharine of Aragon's life had come to a tragic and lonely end.

The first wife of Henry VIII. . .

Born in December, 1485, Katharine was the younger daughter of Ferdinand and Isabella, joint rulers of Castile and Aragon. This formidable royal pair united Spain under their rule and drove the last Islamic ruler from the Iberian peninsular when they took Granada in 1492. She inherited much of their toughness, which she was going to need in later life. In England the new Tudor king, Henry VII, was keen to forge a new alliance with this rising European power. In 1501, aged 15, Katharine was sent to England to marry Arthur, Henry's eldest son, himself a teenager. First impressions were good. Courtier and civil servant Sir Thomas More wrote that Katharine's arrival "thrilled the hearts of everyone, there is nothing lacking in her that the most beautiful girl should have". But within months Arthur was dead. Katharine was left widowed, and in diplomatic limbo. She was betrothed to the younger son, Henry, the 'spare heir'. The two eventually married when the 18-year-old prince became king in 1509. For a while all was well. But Henry VIII was desperate for a male heir to secure his dynasty, and avoid a repeat of the civil wars that had wrecked the country in the previous century. Katharine had a son, but he died; she had a daughter too, Mary, who survived. But Henry needed a boy to succeed him – and that was the root cause of all that followed.

Anne Boleyn and all that. . .

By the later 1520s it was clear Katharine could not give Henry his male heir. It was then Anne Boleyn entered the scene, and Henry tried to persuade the pope to annul his marriage. He claimed the marriage was invalid, as Katharine was his brother's widow. Was he genuine? Hard to say what went through the mind of the tyrant. What is certain was that Katharine would not go quietly, denying her marriage to Arthur had ever been consummated. She was particularly impressive during a trial held in front of papal legates, in which she showed Henry up with her regal manner and dignity. But by 1531 her position was untenable; banished from court her rooms were given to Anne. Henry married a pregnant Anne in 1533. Shortly after that, in May of that year, Katharine's marriage was nullified, and Henry was declared Supreme Head of the English Church. England broke with Rome. For the remaining three years of her life Katharine was adamant she was Henry's legal wife. She stayed loyal to the pope, in the face of increasing pressure.

Any supporters?

Katharine was popular in the country. Most ordinary people saw her as the 'proper' queen, deposed by a usurper with dodgy connections who many suspected of being a witch. Bishop John Fisher and former Chancellor Thomas More were her chief supporters, but both paid with their lives in 1535. Royal authority went a long way; defying Henry got you killed in all sorts of nasty ways, as the rebels of the Pilgrimage of Grace were soon to find out. In the spring of 1534, Katharine was banished to distant Kimbolton Castle, near Huntingdon. A prisoner? Not quite. . . but she was not free to leave. In charge of security was a Norfolk gentleman. Sir Edmund Bedingfeld was the owner of Oxburgh Hall in Norfolk, and had the difficult task of keeping most visitors away from the former queen. He was Steward and Comptroller of her household, such as it was now that she was regarded as the Dowager Princess of Wales – merely the widow of Henry's brother. Most hurtful of all, she was not able to see or even correspond with her daughter Mary, who was enduring her own troubles at court. Katharine kept to one room with a handful of loyal retainers, fasting and leaving only to attend mass. Sympathisers ferried secret messages between mother and daughter. Both could have had better terms, and each other's company, had they acknowledged Anne as queen. Both reacted to that with scorn.

It didn't end well

Katharine's health deteriorated quickly. Within two years she was dead, expiring on January 7, 1536, aged 50. Despite everything she stayed loyal to Henry. On her deathbed, her final letter to the king concluded: "Lastly, I make this vow, that mine eyes desire you above all things." Was it the damp fenland climate that killed her? A broken heart, perhaps? Or, worse, was she poisoned? In the heady atmosphere of the time many thought either Henry or Anne had ordered her killed. Their conduct did little to deflect suspicion. The Venetian ambassador Polydore Vergil recorded that Henry wore yellow when the news reached him – a sign he was not in mourning. Others said Anne did the same. Despite the dark rumours of the time, modern forensic experts suspect cancer was the cause of death. The king did not attend Katharine's funeral, and forbade Mary to go as well. Instead, it was Edmund Bedingfeld who organised a sad, low key procession, on Henry's orders, to the nearest great abbey; Peterborough Cathedral. There Katharine was laid to rest.

What happened next?

Anne Boleyn fell from favour, and was executed in May, 1536. Henry's behaviour became more tyrannical as he aged, unleashing the Reformation on England. In East Anglia, as elsewhere in the country, Katharine's memory was revered. Nearly 20 years later it was people from Norfolk and Suffolk who helped her daughter Mary succeed to the throne; threatened by a coup d'etat in London she rallied troops at Framlingham while the Navy went over to her at Yarmouth. Katharine's tomb was later subjected to the tender mercies of Oliver Cromwell's Ironside troopers during the Civil War. In 1643 they ransacked the cathedral, and made off with the gilding on the letters on the tomb. During the 1700s a Dean of the cathedral is said to have used the black marble of the original tomb in his summer house! In recent times, amends have been made. The queen's tomb in Peterborough Cathedral can be seen and it is often decorated with flowers or pomegranates, her heraldic symbol. It describes her as 'Katharine, Queen of England'. Peterborough is twinned with her birthplace, the Castilian city of Alcala de Henares, and schoolchildren in both Spain and England keep the link active. On the 470th anniversary of her death, in 2006, the Spanish ambassador to Britain attended a special ceremony at the cathedral. The Katharine of Aragon Festival is held in late January at the cathedral; a civic service is held, and children and historical re-enactors dress up in Tudor costumes.

16th century **1560**

Death of Amy Robsart

In 1560 the dead body of a young woman was discovered at the bottom of some stairs in a country house. How Amy Robsart, daughter of a Norfolk squire, died is still a mystery involving Queen Elizabeth I, her noble favourite – and the fate of England.

Who was Amy Robsart?

She was born at Syderstone, near Fakenham, in about 1532. The only legitimate child of Sir John Robsart, she made a glittering marriage aged just 18. Her husband was the dashing Lord Robert Dudley, himself a teenager at the time. Unlike many such marriages, it was a love match. No portrait of Amy survives, but contemporary reports say she was very attractive, and caught the eye of Robert, himself reputedly the best-looking man in the country. They wed at the royal palace at Richmond, attended by King Edward VI and his court. The early days of their marriage were happy, spent largely in Norfolk, where Robert became joint-steward of the Manor of Rising and constable of the castle. But he was a Dudley, and destined for greater things.

Who were the Dudleys?

A thrusting, radical Protestant family on the make. Robert's grandfather had been Henry VII's chief minister, but was beheaded by Henry VIII. The family's fortunes soon rose again. At the time Robert and Amy married, Robert's father was Duke of Northumberland. He was the power behind the throne, and the man who crushed Robert Kett's Norfolk and Norwich rebellion in 1549. The sickly boy king Edward was his ward and did as the Duke commanded. But the Dudleys aimed higher; Northumberland married his son Guilford to Lady Jane Grey, and hoped to inherit the crown through her. When Edward died in 1553 the Dudleys staged a coup d'etat and installed Jane as queen. The coup failed, Northumberland was executed and Robert sent to the Tower.

What about his wife?

Amy was safely at home with her father. She seems to have been a quiet and charming person, happy on a country estate. What she was not was a courtier's wife, and Robert was a courtier through and through. Eventually released, but with his property confiscated, he was not content to live with his wife's relations in Norfolk. Ambition spurred him on to fight in the army at the disastrous siege of Calais in 1558 (England's last remaining possession on the continent was seized by the French) and his prospects seemed dim under Queen Mary. But, in the autumn of 1558, his prayers were answered. Mary died and her half-sister Elizabeth became queen. Dudley's fortunes revived once again. He and Elizabeth had been childhood friends, and soon they would become much more than that.

How much more? Bad news for Lady Dudley. . .

As Robert hastened to court, and was installed as Elizabeth's Master of Horse, his wife stayed in the country. No doubt the rumours soon reached her of the growing infatuation between queen and favourite. Abandon, if you can, the familiar image of the Virgin Queen in her later glory, turning back the Spanish Armada. In 1558 her hold on power was tenuous. During the 16th century the idea of a woman ruler was seen as disastrous, that of an unmarried woman even worse. She was vulnerable. Beset by fears of French invasion, in a country riven by religious dissent and undermined by scheming nobles, Elizabeth needed all the allies she could get. Into this combustible mix strode Robert Dudley. Most observers, contemporary and subsequent, believe Elizabeth and Dudley were lovers and would have married had he been free. He had plenty of enemies, from the queen's Catholic Howard relations to her shrewd chief minister Lord Cecil. Nearly everyone agreed Elizabeth must get married for the security of the country, but surely not to a Dudley. His family's greed, ambition and extreme Protestantism would have divided the nation. Civil war may have broken out had he married Elizabeth, but the affair went on. Robert and Amy met infrequently, and she was shunted off to various relatives in the country. Although she wanted for nothing materially, spending lavishly on clothes, the marriage was a sham. Rumours were rife he was about to divorce her – or worse.

Was he that ruthless?

Let's split facts from speculation. By 1560 Dudley acted like a king in waiting. Spanish ambassador De Quadra called him "the King that is to be". It appeared only the inconvenient Amy stood in his way, and De Quadra reported the queen as saying she was "close to death". In June, 1560, Amy was staying at the house of her husband's friends in Cumnor, Oxfordshire. One day she directed the whole household should visit Abingdon Fair, leaving her alone in the house. Servants returned and found her body at the foot of the stairs. Her neck was broken.

Did she fall or was she pushed?

You can choose your own conspiracy theory. Certainly, she was made miserable by her husband, and had been heard praying for release from life. Suicide was a possibility, leaving Dudley at least morally responsible. But suicide was rare in a religious age in which it was considered a mortal sin. She may have been ill with breast cancer, and porous bones caused by disease may have weakened her. But there were many people who believed she could have been murdered, by either Elizabeth's or Dudley's agents. But they must have known that death in suspicious circumstances would cause a massive scandal, as indeed it did at home and abroad. And were they as amoral as all that? We'd like to think not. A third suspect is Cecil. Did that wily, Machiavellian minister, so determined to ensure Elizabeth stayed securely on the throne, decide an innocent woman must die to discredit Dudley and save England in a greater cause? It's quite a leap to think so, but it is possible. Verdict; unproven. An inquest at Abingdon decided death was accidental, and the tragic Amy was buried at Oxford. Her husband was not present at the funeral, where the minister mistakenly described her as a "lady piteously slain", but Dudley seems to have been genuinely grief-stricken by the death of the girl he had loved years ago.

What happened next?

In Cecil's words Dudley was "infamed by his wife's death" and his hopes of marrying Elizabeth were dead. It didn't stop him enjoying a glittering career as Earl of Leicester and England's leading military commander. When he finally did get married to courtier's widow Lettice Knollys, secretly and without the Queen's permission, Elizabeth was furious (though she did forgive him – eventually). He died in 1588, still Elizabeth's one true love. She, as we know, never married, but became a great ruler, and England gained from that.

16th century **1575**

Waiting for Elizabeth

In the 16th century two Elizabethan grandees spent a small fortune on a house fit to host a queen. The result was an extravagant building project that later went to rack and ruin.

Well, let's hope the queen enjoyed her visit!

Queen Elizabeth I never visited Kirby Hall, near Stamford. Which must have been a huge disappointment to both Sir Humphrey Stafford and Sir Christopher Hatton. Real Renaissance men, both of them pushed the boat out to entice the monarch to pay a visit. Doubly galling was the fact the queen was perfectly happy to stay with their neighbours a few miles down the road. Stafford was one of those 'new men' who came to prominence under the Tudors. Rising to wealth in the 1540s he inherited former monastic land, and began to build on it. Appointed Sheriff of Northamptonshire in 1566, he needed a property that would reflect his standing. A village, complete with church, had stood there, but it was nearly deserted by this time. Stafford demolished church and houses and made an architectural statement. This man had style, and he wanted everyone to know it. By the latter part of the 16th century novel ideas about building were coming into England from the continent. French and Italian architects were in vogue. Kirby Hall was going to be all about perfect symmetry and decoration. Work got under way in 1570.

What about the neighbours?

It was an age of conspicuous consumption. A few miles to the north William Cecil, Lord Burghley, was busily constructing his enormous Burghley House. To the west Elizabeth's favourite Robert Dudley, Earl of Leicester, was upgrading Kenilworth. Stafford died in 1575. Kirby was bought by 35-year-old Sir Christopher Hatton. He was one of the queen's leading courtiers, and had quickly caught her eye with his skill at dancing. This "comely young man" enjoyed a meteoric rise to power, becoming Lord Chancellor and a Knight of the Garter. Later he helped fund Francis Drake's voyage around the world. The name of Drake's famous ship, The Golden Hind, was inspired by Hatton's

English country garden: The gardens at Kirby Hall have been restored to the days of their 17th century splendour.

family insignia, incorporating a hind. Kirby was built to impress. From the ornate porch, complete with intricate decorations full of symbolism an educated Elizabethan would understand, it drew the visitor in via a superbly symmetrical courtyard. Inside, on the ground floor was a great hall, complete with minstrels' gallery. In its heyday, musicians would have entertained the household. Upstairs, visitors could not fail to be impressed by the long gallery. Covered from the elements, the family could stroll along this walkway enjoying fine portraits and tapestries hung there. Further in, the state room led to one great guestroom. Built for luxury and commanding outstanding views of the garden, it was intended for the queen herself. Despite this, Hatton spent more time and even more money at his nearby property at Holdenby. Although the queen was at one time reputed to be his lover (unlikely!) she never visited either house.

Why didn't she come?

She was busy. A kingdom to run, Armadas to fight . . . yet Elizabeth went on many progresses during her reign. The whole court went with her, an entourage up to 2,000 strong. In 1578 her progress took her through East Anglia, staying at homes in Cambridgeshire, Suffolk and Norfolk. On other occasions she stayed at nearby Deene Park and with Burghley at Stamford but Kirby, for some reason, missed out. Hatton spent all his considerable wealth on his houses. He died in 1591, spectacularly in debt and childless, and his nephew inherited. Another Christopher (known as No II to differentiate him from three others sharing the same Christian name) he had better luck with royal visits. James I inherited the crown after Elizabeth's death in 1603, and liked Kirby so much he came four times, along with his queen, Anne of Denmark. On these occasions, in 1612, 1616, 1619 and 1624 the whole government of England revolved around this house. The great state rooms finally fulfilled their original purpose.

Nothing to worry about then. . .

The following generation had little luck. Christopher Hatton III supported the king during the Civil War. At the end of hostilities he had to flee a victorious and vengeful Parliament, but ended up in comfortable exile in France. His wife Elizabeth was left to run the estate in his absence. It was a hard time as she had no income. Before long, in increasing debt, she didn't even have enough cash to clothe the children. In 1655 she wrote to her husband "all ye poor children are well though stark naked Charles with only half a shirt. . ." Her neighbours rallied round, with gifts of plum pudding, but the estate got into debt. After the Restoration their fortunes improved for a while. Her son became Christopher Hatton IV when he inherited. His work on the garden meant that for a brief time it was regarded by those in the know as "ye best in England". Glory proved fleeting. After Hatton IV's death the estate declined. It stayed in the family, but they had big houses elsewhere they preferred. By the 19th century Kirby was in a bad way. In places the roof had caved in, walls were falling down and a family of shepherds was living in the old servants' quarters and a farm hand in the library. From romantic ruin to condemned wreck was the next step. By 1932, when it came into government hands, it was crumbling away – but rescue was at hand.

What's there today?

Kirby Hall is hidden away in rolling countryside. A programme of renovation by English Heritage has rescued most of the state rooms, though parts are still a shell. The gardens have been restored to their 17th century pomp. In 1998 a film company used it to film scenes for a version of Jane Austen's novel Mansfield Park. Kirby Hall is also home to some wonderfully flamboyant and vocal peacocks. Like the original owners, they would surely be happy to subscribe to the motto: "If you've got it, flaunt it!"

16th century **1593**

Warboys witches

The "most momentous" witchcraft trial in history took place in the Fenland village of Warboys towards the end of the reign of Queen Elizabeth I.

What, bigger than the Salem witchhunts?

In 1593 Alice Samuel, her husband and daughter were tried and executed for witchcraft in Warboys. Historians believe the case set the template for the witch-hunts that took place over the next century or so in England and its colonies. The Salem trial took place a century later, and has entered folklore, largely thanks to Arthur Miller's play The Crucible, based on events that shook England's American colonies. The seeds for that tragedy were sown in the Mother Country.

Superstitious nonsense?

Witchcraft was nothing new in England – and people believed in it from top to bottom of society. Thomas Browne, the Norwich doctor and intellectual, was a rational man with tolerant views on most subjects – but he believed witchcraft was a reality. Similarly, King James I was famous for his learning – but he was among the most enthusiastic witch-hunters in British history. Norfolk judge Edward Coke defined a witch as "a person that hath conference with the Devil to consult with him or to do some act". Witchcraft was known and feared throughout the Middle Ages, and there were laws and popular religious remedies against it. However, witchcraft was not all evil. 'Cunning' men and women were respected in country areas and people went to them for their skill in healing, for example. On the continent though, witch-hunters were becoming increasingly aggressive. The papal bull *Malleus Maleficarum* of 1485 defined the offence, and led to increased persecution.

And in England?

During the 16th and 17th centuries society changed. Protestantism suppressed folk superstitions and was hostile to old, pagan ways. Historian Keith Thomas, author of the ground-breaking 1970s work Religion and the Decline of Magic, felt the seeds of persecution lay in this disrupted society. The Reformation led to more individualistic economic practices and a break-up of traditional village charity given to the poor. People living at the margins of society became objects of suspicion. These included elderly, poor women, often widows living alone or perhaps with a cat for company. When something went wrong – a child becoming ill, cattle dying, milk going off, bad weather – a scapegoat needed finding. The defenceless and friendless, people who may have a grudge against the better-off, were suspected.

What happened in Warboys?

In 1589 squire Robert Throckmorton moved to Warboys. He lived with his family in the manor house near the village church. Robert was well-connected, a friend of Sir Henry Cromwell, among the leading men in the county. That November Throckmorton's 10-year-old daughter Jane started suffering from fits. To add to the family's worries Jane's four sisters started to show similar symptoms. After his original prescriptions failed to work, Cambridge physician Dr Burrows suggested sorcery was at work. Suspicion fell on impoverished 76-year-old neighbour Alice Samuel, who Jane accused of being a witch. The following spring Lady Cromwell, grandmother of Oliver Cromwell, visited Warboys. She openly accused Alice of witchcraft. After arguing with her she took a pair of scissors and cut off a lock of Alice's hair which she gave to the girls' distraught mother to burn. This was a popular remedy to ward off witchcraft. Alice denied the charges, saying: "Madam, why do you use me thus? I never did you any harm as yet."

As yet?

The words came back to haunt her. Lady Cromwell suffered nightmares and illness, and died two years later. The Throckmorton girls now accused Alice Samuels of her murder. In a misguided move to solve matters, she moved in with the family as it was felt only she could prevent the girls' fits, from which they eventually recovered, and ceased their allegations. But things had gone too far. The village vicar persuaded a browbeaten Alice to confess to witchcraft. Although she immediately retracted the confession, she was brought before the Bishop of Lincoln, and again confessed. Contrary to popular opinion, torture was forbidden to secure a confession, though mental pressures such as denial of sleep were brought to bear. Alice's husband John and daughter Agnes were implicated, and all three were arrested and

The village sign at Tilney All Saints reflects the wonderful tale of Tom Hickathrift, the Fenland Giant. Was he a real man, who lived at the time of the Norman Conquest, or is he just another legend?

Sir Thomas Erpingham, from north Norfolk, commanded the English and Welsh archers at Agincourt in 1415. His statue stands above the Erpingham Gate entrance to Norwich Cathedral.

St Felix was sent by the pope to help convert the pagan Anglo-Saxons of eastern England. His symbol was of a cat's head, which you can see in this medieval carving at Castle Rising in west Norfolk.

The ruins of Castle Acre priory in Norfolk are testament to the break with the past that happened in England during the 1530s, when Henry VIII authorised the dissolution of the monasteries. Here we see the nave of the priory church displaying the vestiges of its once ornate decorations.

The grave of Queen Katharine of Aragon in Peterborough Cathedral. She was buried there following her death in January, 1536.

Religious reformer Thomas Bilney was one of the heretics executed at Lollards Pit in Norwich. He was burnt to death there in 1531.

If you've got it, flaunt it would be an ideal motto for the Elizabethan grandees who built Kirby Hall, in Northamptonshire. Here a modern day peacock in the grounds maintains that fine tradition.

In 1593 the fenland village of Warboys was at the centre of a notorious witch trial. Today this weather vane stands in the village, keeping alive the story of the Warboys Witches.

Sir Robert Mansel fought a famous duel in the Ber Street area of Norwich in the autumn of 1600.

Sudbury's most famous son Thomas Gainsborough captured the spirit of an age, as well as the rolling East Anglian countryside, in his 1748 portrait of Mr and Mrs Andrews.

Wisbech man Thomas Clarkson fought long and hard in the anti-slavery cause, alongside William Wilberforce, during the late 18th and early 19th centuries. This statue in his home town honours his memory. His brother John, a Royal Navy officer, was another anti-slaver.

Boxer Jem Mace was born in Beeston, Norfolk, and led a long and colourful life. This blue plaque in Swan Lane, Norwich, marks his time in charge of the White Swan pub.

Railway contractor Samuel Morton Peto played a vital role in bringing the railways to East Anglia during the mid-19th century. This bust of him is in Norwich Thorpe Railway Station.

In the spring of 1643 Crowland, in the Lincolnshire Fens, was besieged by Oliver Cromwell's Parliamentarians. The town's iconic abbey was one of the places bombarded. Here is a picture of a re-enactment of the siege carried out by members of the Sealed Knot. Picture: Rusty Aldwinckle, www.mistresswinckle.co.uk

Marjorie, Laurie and Ivy Skeats – the author's aunt, uncle and mother – were among thousands of children evacuated from the east end of London to country areas of East Anglia in September, 1939. For all of them, it was a formative experience, and many settled in the area.

The walls of the Roman town Venta Icenorum, near modern Norwich, were built quite late in its history. This is one of the remaining fragments of what was once a thriving settlement.

imprisoned in nearby Huntingdon. The allegations were hard to deny once people were convinced of their guilt. Hysteria grew. A jailer who chained Alice to a bedpost fell ill. Therefore, it had to be witchcraft. On April 5, 1593, the Samuels were found guilty of the murder by witchcraft of Lady Cromwell. Alice's portentous words "as yet" were vital in securing the conviction. They were hanged. Lady Cromwell's husband used £40 raised from the Samuels' confiscated property to pay for a sermon preached annually against witchcraft in Huntingdon. It continued until 1812.

What happened next?

Historian George Kittredge said the Warboys trial was "the most momentous that had ever occurred in England. It produced a deep and lasting impression on the class that made laws". Lord Chief Justice Anderson declared in 1602: "The land is full of witches." Two years later a new Witchcraft Bill was passed. This increased persecution against witches, introducing the death penalty even if a victim was merely injured. The eastern counties seemed particularly afflicted; in the 1640s the individual who called himself 'Witchfinder General', Matthew Hopkins, took advantage of the disruption created by civil war to terrorise East Anglia by launching a campaign against witches in which hundreds died. Hopkins was a genuinely nasty piece of work, portrayed by the actor Vincent Price in the 1968 film Witchfinder General (trashy, fictionalised, but worth a watch, though quite disturbing). Appropriately enough, it seems his reign of terror only ended when he was himself accused of – and executed for – witchcraft.

Poetic justice. When did belief in witchcraft finally die out?

By 1692 educated people were increasingly sceptical. Popular belief survived longer. The infamous Salem trial of that year in New England followed the same pattern as that in Warboys; young girls suffering hysterical fits, neighbourly falling-outs and suspicion in a tight-knit community leading to accusation. The last recorded hanging for witchcraft in England was in 1685 (this date is disputed), the legislation only repealed in 1735. Lynchings and violence in rural areas went on into the 19th century. In some parts of the world belief in witchcraft remains vibrant. Today, the people of Warboys are rather proud of their witches. Its Victorian clock tower features a weather vane depicting a witch, while a witch on a broomstick has been part of the logo of the primary school for many years.

17th century **1600**

The Ber Street duel

In October 1600 two men met in a deadly duel outside Norwich's Ber Street gates. The result was a severed limb, and a scrap that went down in Norfolk legend.

Just another typical Norwich night out?

They were known as the 'Fighting Heydons'. Members of this distinguished Norfolk family were never backward when it came to a scrap. In the case of the duel between Sir John Heydon and Sir Robert Mansel, the matter reached the ears of the highest officers of state, who sought to stop the duel from happening.

Why was it so important?

The actual cause of the duel is a little hazy, but it seems likely it was pegged to the waning fortunes of the Earl of Essex, Robert Devereux. He had once been Queen Elizabeth's favourite, but his ambitious nature and military failure in Ireland had lost him that status. The Heydon brothers – Christopher and John – were keen supporters of Essex. John had accompanied the Earl to Ireland, and had been knighted by him. But in the autumn of 1600 Christopher and John were careering down a path that would lead them to public disgrace, bankruptcy and – in John's case – mutilation. The immediate cause of their troubles was Sir Robert Mansel.

Who was he?

Originally from Wales, Mansel (sometimes the name is spelt, confusingly, as Mansfield) was a seafarer. Born in about 1573, he was a courageous Elizabethan 'sea dog' who married the widow of a Norfolk squire who had property at Pentney, near King's Lynn. This led him to take an interest in the county's politics, which sowed the seeds of problems to come. Before that Mansel's career led him to Spain and one of the most successful overseas expeditions of the Elizabethan era. England had been at war with Spain since the defeat of the Armada in 1588 – but this was far from the end of hostilities.

In 1596 the Earl of Essex led an assault on Cadiz. This was the home port of the still powerful Spanish fleet. Mansel, then in his mid-twenties, was the captain of HMS Vanguard. Essex and Norfolk admiral Charles Howard of Effingham gathered a powerful force, with Sir Walter Raleigh commanding a squadron; 150 ships with 7,000 soldiers and volunteers and 6,500 sailors, sailed from Plymouth, joined by 20 ships from England's Dutch allies. The attack was wholly successful. The Spanish fleet was burnt at anchor and the English sacked Cadiz. Mansel was knighted for his part.

A man on the rise?

Sir Robert looked to make his mark on Norfolk politics, standing for parliament as county MP (knight of the shire). But he was seen as an interloper, and clashed with the Heydons. It's possible the Heydons' support for the Earl of Essex may have played a part in the argument. By the autumn of 1600, Essex was plotting against Elizabeth. Mansel and others, such as Sir John Townshend, of Raynham Hall, stayed loyal to the queen. It was therefore no coincidence that October when Christopher Heydon challenged Townshend to a duel, while brother John faced Mansel.

If the boys want to fight, you gotta let them. . .

In London the privy council took a hard line. They detained Christopher in London, and prevented his duel. The Lord Chief Justice wrote to the queen's chief minister, Sir Robert Cecil, warning him to stop the Mansel-Heydon clash, since Norfolk was "already too much wrought into faction". Too late. On October 9 the fight took place. It was a bad-tempered affair, without the usual polite formalities, and the seconds were banished out of sight. Mansel, impatient to be at it, fought with a rapier an inch shorter than Heydon's rather than wait for another. Both were wounded quickly, Heydon more seriously. By Mansel's account, Heydon cried for quarter, but then attacked him. . ."when he was up, without speaking any one word, he ran me into the breast again, and my thrust missed him. Then we fell to stabs with our daggers." Mansel claimed Heydon, having been "mauled severely" eventually laid down his weapons. Heydon's hand was severed, probably after the fight was over, and is now in a mummified state on display in Norwich Castle Museum. Mansel was also wounded, and his career briefly suffered, but he recovered. In February, 1601 Essex raised his followers in a chaotic rising in London. The Heydon brothers led troops through Ludgate. The rebellion quickly fizzled out, and Essex was executed; the Heydons were lucky to escape with their lives, but their public careers were over and they had huge fines to pay. Both Mansel and Townshend, significantly, took an active role in rounding up Essex's followers.

A successful career?

Mansel's role in the Norwich duel counted against him locally, and he was defeated in the 1601 county election, but was elected as King's Lynn MP. His naval career continued, as he became Vice Admiral of the Narrow Seas in 1603 and Treasurer of the Navy the following year. His later exploits included chasing pirates from Algiers and financing an expedition to find the North-West Passage from North America to the Pacific Ocean; there is a Mansel Island in the Hudson Strait. He revolutionised glass manufacture, importing Venetian glassmakers and setting up a glass factory in Newcastle. He pioneered the use of sea coal rather than wood in the manufacturing process, and created a monopoly. This made him new enemies (as if he needed any more!) He was accused of dishonesty as an administrator, which led to brief imprisonment in 1618. In Norwich he lived in the Committee House in Bethel Street between 1596 and 1603, and died in London in 1656.

Anything else?

Sir John Townshend's luck ran out in 1603 when he fought a duel on Hounslow Heath against Sir Matthew Browne. Browne died at the scene, while Townshend died the following day. On a happier note, the English soldiers and sailors who sacked Cadiz in 1596 came away with barrels of vino de Jerez, known to us as sherry. The enduring English taste for this fine fortified wine had begun!

My thanks to Peter Mansel James, of Norwich, for information on his distant forebear.

Jacob Astley's prayer

Oh Lord, thou knowest how busy I must be this day. If I forget thee, do not thou forget me.

A soldier's prayer?

Sir Jacob Astley was a professional soldier, born in Norfolk to a family of long-established gentry. By the time civil war broke out in England in 1642, and he led inexperienced troops into battle, he was one of the few protagonists who really knew what warfare was all about. A staunch Royalist from a county which backed Parliament, Astley was born at Melton Constable in 1579, and spent most of his adult life fighting, from the Azores islands in the mid-Atlantic to Bohemia in central Europe – and, of course, in England. He had the distinction of producing the best-known quote at the start of the first Civil War – and having the last word four years later.

Wasn't a soldier's life an unattractive proposition for a gentleman?

Far from it. An officer could profit greatly from a long war. During the Thirty Years War in Europe (1618-48) professional soldiers could make a good living and, with luck, retire on the proceeds. Many fought in the English Civil War out of conviction and loyalty, but many came because it was their job. The plain-speaking Jacob Astley was one of the more principled members of the profession. He first saw action in 1597. Aged 18, he joined the Earl of Essex and Sir Walter Raleigh, in an expedition against the then Spanish-held Azores islands. He saw service under the Dutch Prince Maurice of Nassau, then allied with England against the Spanish empire, and became one of his officers at the battle of Nieuport (1600). With no standing army in England at the time Astley stayed soldiering in Europe. He married Dutchwoman Agnes Impel, with whom he had two sons and a daughter. By 1621 his career was to take a new turn as went to the rescue of the 'winter queen'. Princess Elizabeth was the daughter of James I of England, and sister of the future Charles I. She had married Frederick, the Elector Palatine in Bohemia, whose kingdom (now the Czech Republic) was under attack by the Catholic Holy Roman Empire. Astley took part in the dramatic mid-winter rescue of the royal family as Prague fell to the imperialists. As a reward he joined their household and became tutor in military affairs to their son. He was Prince Rupert of the Rhine – and their futures were about to become entwined.

The English Civil War

Astley fought for the Protestant side under Dutch and Danish command in the vicious Thirty Years War struggles on the continent during the 1630s. In England they were relieved to avoid the ruinous religious warfare that scarred Europe. That was about to change. By the late 1630s Charles I was under pressure in England, and had lost control of Scotland due to his religious policy. Desperate to raise an army, terminally short of cash and lacking competent generals, he turned to Astley, and appointed him Sergeant-Major-General of the army to face the Scots in 1639. Astley was appalled at the state of the forces he commanded, and bluntly warned the king they were not up to scratch. Unsurprisingly the unpaid, untrained demoralised army was shattered by the Scots. Within three years Charles faced open rebellion in England – and the armies blundered into each other at Edgehill in the Midlands in October, 1642.

Time to say a prayer?

Charles I's court was riven by dissent and self-seeking flattery. Astley was a fish out of water in the king's councils, but his European experience and reputation for discipline and honesty saw him command the Royalist infantry while his protege, the dashing Rupert, led the Cavalier cavalry. Astley uttered his famous prayer as he led his men forward at Edgehill. The battle opened with a charge by Rupert's horsemen that swept the Parliamentarian cavalry from the field – but they then disappeared in an undisciplined search for loot. Astley's foot, deprived of cavalry support, were soon enmeshed in a vicious infantry melée as pikemen and musketeers clashed. His opposite number in the Parliamentary ranks was Philip Skippon, from Foulsham in Norfolk. As the general had warned, the poorly trained soldiers on both sides were unable to attain victory. Edgehill was a bloody draw, and ushered in years of civil war. With the country divided, East Anglia, including Astley's native Norfolk, was dominated by Parliament. Astley stayed loyal to Charles, fought bravely at places like Gloucester and Newbury, and became Baron Astley of Reading in 1644. The outcome of the war was still in the balance at this time, but the following year saw Parliament reform its army and create a force capable of making a difference.

The New Model Army?

This redcoated army was still an untried force when the two sides clashed at Naseby in June, 1645. Astley led his infantry well, and initially had the New Model on the run. Victory looked possible, until Oliver Cromwell's disciplined 'Ironside' cavalry hit them in the flanks. In the ensuing rout the Royalist infantry that Astley had built up was virtually destroyed. On the Parliamentary side, the able Philip Skippon held a similar rank in the New Model Army, and led the centre of the line. With Rupert failing to hold on to the vital port of Bristol, the king was besieged at his Oxford headquarters. Just one field army remained, led by Astley. After Naseby he commanded the king's remaining troops in Wales. Eventually he was able to raise 3,000 men and in spring, 1646, marched to Charles's rescue. It was not to be. At Stow-on-the-Wold he was defeated in the last battle of the war. Surrendering, he told his Parliamentarian captors: "Well, boys, you have done your work, now you may go and play – if you don't fall out among yourselves".

Prophetic words

Soon the victors were indeed falling out among themselves. A second war broke out in 1648, including a particularly brutal 11-week siege of Royalist-held Colchester by Parliament. It resulted in two of the Royalist commanders being summarily shot by a firing squad after the town was stormed. The following year Charles I was put on trial and subsequently beheaded. Astley, now in his late sixties, took no part in it, having given his word not to fight again. This did not stop him being imprisoned, but eventually he was able to live in retirement at Maidstone (Norfolk being an uncomfortable spot for beaten Royalists). He died early in 1652. Philip Skippon also led a relatively quiet life. Although named as one of King Charles I's judges at his trial in 1649, he took the pragmatic decision not to attend the trial. A wise decision; many of the regicides who put the monarch to death were imprisoned or executed after the Restoration of 1660. Skippon became MP for King's Lynn under Oliver Cromwell's Commonwealth of the 1650s. He died early in 1660, a few months before Charles II returned to England as king.

17th century **1643**

The siege of Crowland

Simmering fenland rivalries between neighbours and wartime politics led to a siege in the spring of 1643.

The towns of Spalding and Crowland lie a few miles apart in the Lincolnshire fens. This normally quiet, isolated part of the country exploded into hostage-taking and violence early in the English Civil War. It attracted the attention of none other than Oliver Cromwell.

By the sword divided?

War had broken out between King Charles I and Parliament the previous year, but by the early months of 1643 stalemate had ensued. Both sides were busy raising professional forces, but many of the participants were still enthusiastic amateurs. Crowland, famed for its medieval abbey, stood on the northern edge of territory controlled by the Eastern Association. It was Parliamentary country, but with Royalist armies fighting in the midlands and the north, opinions were divided. Into this combustible mix marched one Captain Welby. Originally described as a "gentleman" from the nearby village of Gedney Hill, he allied with his fellow Royalist, the Rev William Styles, vicar of Crowland, to persuade people there to support King Charles. According to his critics, whose views we must take with a pinch of salt, he was "a most irreligious roarer and railer against all goodness". In neighbouring Spalding, puritan minister Mr Robert Ram, was alarmed. He wrote to the people of Crowland in their Royalist island, warning them against the course they had taken.

A good move?

The last thing people in Crowland wanted was their uppity neighbours telling them what to do. Styles and Welby, along with a raiding party of about 80 men, descended on undefended Spalding on March 24. They kidnapped Ram from his parsonage, along with a leading citizen, John Harrington, and three others, and took them back to Crowland in triumph. The hostages were kept under guard by Captain Thomas Styles (perhaps the vicar of Crowland's brother). Meanwhile, the Crowlanders beefed up their defences, in the form of earthworks including trenches and bulwarks around the abbey. Welby also built three forts over a mile out along each of three causeways that controlled the only access to the town. Spring flooding in the isolated fens ensured these were the only feasible routes into the town. Crowland was a natural fortress.

What was happening in Spalding?

If took three weeks for Spaldonians to mount a rescue mission. They appealed for help from Parliament. A detachment of 'Norfolk blades' arrived, under Colonel Miles Hobart. They were part of a regiment being raised in Peterborough by an energetic Ely landowner turned cavalry commander – Oliver Cromwell. The Spalding men jumped the gun by attacking the outlying forts early on April 13. According to Robert Ram's account, the only surviving eye-witness story of the siege, the hostages were taken "down to the bulwark upon the North side of the town, and kept there among the rude soldiers". There was a stand-off, but both sides withdrew. Was there an element of traditional inter-town showing-off, rather than real martial intent on both sides? The events of the following day were far more serious. Captain William Dodson, one of Cromwell's men from Wisbech, arrived with his troops. He sent a drummer boy as a messenger, carrying a summons to surrender. The Crowlanders broke the rules of warfare by taking him prisoner.

Things were getting nasty. . .

The hostages were placed deliberately in harm's way. Ram wrote: "All five of us were set upon the top of the breastwork where we stood fast for three hours, our friends shooting fiercely at us. . . before they recognised us. Captain Harrington took one of his soldiers' muskets. . . and himself made three shots at his own father." Fortunately, their aim was not very good. Civil war firearms were notoriously inaccurate at distance. "The Crowland works were very strong, and well-lined with musketeers who were backed with store of hassock knives, long scythes, and such-like fennish weapons". The defences held. The Crowlanders celebrated this victory "in revelling and drinking". Their celebrations were premature. Stung by these early reverses, a formidable Parliamentary force was assembled. Cromwell joined the assault, advancing along the west bank from Peakirk with his Ironsides – a regiment of horse, foot and deadly artillery. Along with a troop of dragoons (mounted infantry) from Boston, the attacking force numbered more than 2,000 against about 200 defenders. To counter the tactic of using the hostages as 'human shields' again Cromwell's men made it clear they would show no quarter to the Crowlanders if they persisted. Although in subsequent attacks Ram was taken to the front line, he was not placed on the bulwarks again. Bad weather delayed the final attack, but the attackers continued to harass the defenders in their causeway forts. By Thursday, April 27, Cromwell's artillery was able to pound both the forts and the town, including the abbey. The noise and terror of destructive cannon balls landing in their midst, particularly with their homes and families threatened, must have damaged the defenders' morale. Most of them were, after all, inexperienced citizen soldiers. Ram recorded: "They so played the Croylanders upon every quarter that their hearts began to fail. Divers of them stole away into the coverts and marshy ground on the east side of the town. . ." Among many deserters was Captain Welby, who disappeared at this point. Organised defence was breaking down.

Time to wave the white flag?

Styles's attempts to secure treaty terms failed when Cromwell and the other Parliamentary commanders tore up the paper they were written on. Hundreds of troops then overran the shattered earthworks and poured into the town. By the time they reached the abbey, its defences had been abandoned. The siege was over. Casualties were mercifully light, with six men dying; one defender and five attackers. The hostages were freed and went home. Parliament garrisoned Crowland for the following year. Royalist hopes in the region were in tatters by 1644, though the king's forces retained control of the Lincolnshire fortress of Newark. Cromwell went on to fight in the Lincolnshire area at Burghley House and Grantham, as well as contributing to the Parliamentarian siege of King's Lynn. At the Battle of Marston Moor in Yorkshire, fought in the summer of 1644, he and his Ironsides announced themselves on the national stage.

What's there now?

Crowland is something of a hidden gem in the south Lincolnshire fens. The ruins of the abbey and its thriving modern church continue to dominate the flat landscape for miles around – an iconic, rather beautiful, sight for travellers and artists to enjoy. Guides welcome visitors to the abbey seven days a week. In recent years the Sealed Knot has recreated the events of the siege in colourful re-enactments each September.

Diary of an iconoclast

An iconoclast. In other words, a mindless vandal who destroyed beautiful works of religious art?

William Dowsing was anything but mindless. As for being a vandal, he would say that which he destroyed was wicked, and that he did God's work. This 17th century Suffolk farmer, an enthusiastic Puritan by inclination and practice, left churches in Suffolk and Cambridgeshire changed forever during his nine-month visits from 1643 to 1644. William Dowsing was empowered by a Puritan-dominated Parliament to rid the Church of what was termed superstitious and idolatrous images at the height of the first Civil War.

Why did the Puritans hate such images?

Ever since the Reformation of the previous century England had been split between those who wished to rid – ie 'purify' – the Church of England of its remaining Catholic 'Papist' vestiges. Their Protestantism was one of aural rather than visual imagery; of logic and a personal relationship with God rather than the mystery and magic of Catholicism. Under King Edward VI and his half-sister Elizabeth I much of this work had already been carried out throughout the country. But the Church of England remained an uncomfortable compromise, a half-way house between out-and-out Puritanism and Catholicism. Puritans suspected King Charles I of being a secret Catholic, and Archbishop of Canterbury William Laud's 'High Church' policy of reviving religious imagery inflamed the situation. Much of the ferocity of the Civil War stemmed from this fanaticism.

Dowsing was a convinced Puritan, no doubt

He was born in Laxton in Suffolk in 1596, the younger son of a yeoman farmer. We have very little personal information about him, apart from the usual marriage and death records, but he did leave one indelible legacy. During his brief emergence on the public scene he kept a detailed record proudly recalling every church he visited, what he did and ordered and the people with whom he disagreed. This journal shows how committed he was to the cause. Well educated, his extensive library (where his journal was discovered during the following century) was full of religious tracts demonstrating his radical leanings. He and wife Thamar gave their children Old Testament names – clearly influenced by close reading of the Bible. He was not a man to forget any kind of slight. As he wrote to clergyman Edward Newcomen in Dedham: *"I cannot but take it ill that in two yeerses space you return not my book I lent you on Church Policy."*

An East Anglian landowner with an attitude. Any connection to Oliver Cromwell?

Did they know each other? Surely their paths must have crossed. They were certainly contemporaries; Cromwell was just three years younger than Dowsing. Dowsing was closely acquainted with the Earl of Manchester, one of the leading Parliamentarian army commanders, but as Cromwell and the Earl didn't get on well, they may not have been friendly. Dowsing probably felt the same way Cromwell did during the 1630s; despairing at the 'ungodliness' of the country. In 1640, following his wife's death, Dowsing moved to Stratford St Mary in the Stour Valley, a Puritan stronghold. When war broke out two years later there was no doubt where his loyalties would lie.

Did he join the army?

In summer 1643 a Dowsing is recorded as the Earl of Manchester's Provost-Marshal at the siege of Lynn. Was it our man? We're not sure, but as it was Manchester who gave him his church mission it is tempting to think so. On December 19, 1643, Dowsing was commissioned by Parliament to visit churches in Suffolk and Cambridgeshire to seek out and destroy "monuments of idolatry and superstition". He started straight away. Accompanied by soldiers he made for Pembroke College, Cambridge. Stained glass was either smashed or removed, monumental brass inscriptions ripped up along with altar rails, crucifixes and crosses.

Was there any resistance?

Armed solders usually settle any arguments, but Dowsing was willing to debate the issue with all comers. As it was, he had a lot of local support. Some churchwardens and constables were enthusiastic iconoclasts. Soon Dowsing, overwhelmed by the scale of the task, was delegating work to subordinates. Let him tell the tale in his own words through one excerpt from his journal.

"Beckles [Beccles], April 6. Jehovahs between church and chancel; and the sun over it; and by the altar. My meat is flesh indeed, and My bloods drink indeed. And 2 crosses we gave order to take down, one was on the porch; another on the steeple; and many superstitious pictures, about 40. Six several crosses, Christs, Virgin Marys, St Georges and 3 more; and 13 crosses in all; and Jesus and Mary, in letters; and twelve Apostles."

Between December 21, 1643, and September 26, 1644, Dowsing visited 100 churches in Cambridgeshire and 150 in Suffolk. His writ ran out at the Isle of Ely. The commission ended when Manchester was outmanoeuvred in Parliament by Cromwell, after which Dowsing returned to obscurity.

What happened in Norfolk?

The job there went to a mysterious figure named Captain Clement Gilley (or Gelle, Gille or Gylly, according to different spellings) who visited churches at Banham, Bressingham and Harling. Unlike William Dowsing he left no journals and we only have individual church records to go from. In Norwich Bishop Joseph Hall suffered at the hands of iconoclastic visitors, and many images were destroyed at the city's cathedral. A Committee of Sequestration, led by Yarmouth MP Miles Corbet (of whom more in the next chapter), seized the bishop's palace and goods in 1643. He and his family were evicted. The bishop chronicled his woes in a tract called Hard Measure. After the Parliamentarians had seized the Palace, and smashed the windows, he declared: "They were not ashamed, after they had taken away all my goods and personal estate, to come for me for assessments and monthly payments for that estate which they had taken . . . they had left me nothing." His health failing, he was attended by the celebrated Norwich doctor Thomas Browne, who later paid tribute to "my honoured friend; a person of singular humility, patience and piety".

What did Dowsing do after the war?

He went back home to farming. In 1647 he married Mary Cooper (he was now 57 years old) and the couple had five more children, who were still living in Stratford in the early 18th century. Surprisingly perhaps, he was horrified by the execution of Charles I in 1649 and refused to pledge loyalty to Cromwell's Commonwealth. This counted against him when he later went to court at Ipswich and tried to recover some debts. He died in 1668, no doubt true to his beliefs.

17th century **1662**

Corbet the king killer

I am now on dying ground. I have finished my course. . . and have endeavoured to keep the faith.

With these words Miles Corbet, Puritan stalwart and Great Yarmouth MP, prepared for a gruesome death in April, 1662.

He had no regrets

Regrets did not enter into the mind of a man so firm in his convictions. Miles Corbet was a lawyer, unforgiving in pursuit of his Royalist enemies while in power. The only Norfolk man to sign the death warrant for King Charles I, his resolve never wavered. Yet Corbet came from a family split in two by the divisions of the Civil War. Born at Sprowston, near Norwich, in 1595, he was the younger son of Sir Thomas Corbet. After studying law he became recorder of Yarmouth in 1625 and MP soon afterwards. Some accounts say he did legal work for Oliver Cromwell.

He lived in troubled times

Around the time Miles was establishing himself in Yarmouth – his house was just off the Market Place and later became the Weavers' Arms – his uncle was busy making a name for himself. Clement Corbet was a strict High Churchman, and became the Chancellor of the Norwich Diocese under the Puritan-hating Bishop Wren. His views would put him in direct conflict with his nephew, whose fellow Puritans he hated with a vengeance. Historian R W Ketton-Cremer described both men as sharing "a biting tongue and inquisitorial temper". Clement's views later got him in trouble as Norfolk veered towards Puritanism during the 1630s. Miles was elected as one of the MPs for the borough of Yarmouth in 1639 as king and Parliament embarked on a collision course that led to war within three years.

No doubt he was on Parliament's side

Corbet was active in the affairs of what has been dubbed the Long Parliament.

In June, 1642, two months before Charles raised his standard at Nottingham, Corbet had donated £50 to help pay for horse, plate and armour for Parliamentary forces. As the country divided he was chairman of the Committee for Information and Sequestrations as well as maintaining links with Norfolk. East Anglia was dominated by what was known as the Eastern Association, and declared for Parliament. Known Royalists, such as the L'Estranges of Hunstanton, were harried. Corbet, a "grim-faced, swarthy, saturnine" character was especially hated and feared for his harshness. One Royalist, Clement Walker, characterised him as "this Inquisitor General, this prologue to the hangman who looks more like the hangman himself". When the elderly Bishop of Norwich, Joseph Hall, was deprived of his income local Parliamentarians were inclined to allow him a fifth of his living. Not so Miles Corbet in London, who made sure the old man was evicted from his crumbling palace.

His God was a vengeful one. . .

The way he saw it, he was about God's business. Royalists were "malignants", bishops were anathema and Charles Stuart was a "man of blood" to fervent Puritans like Corbet. He was very much of his time. The Civil War became more bitter as it went on, and the Corbets were not the only Norfolk family split by it; Miles's nephew Sir Thomas fought for the king from start to finish. As views hardened with the defeat of the king, and later outbreak of a second war, so did Corbet's pursuit of beaten Royalists. In 1643 Lynn had been seized in the name of the king by, among others, Sir Hamon L'Estrange. When the town surrendered to the Earl of Manchester it was on favourable terms which stated none of the defenders would be penalised. Corbet succeeded to the role of recorder of Lynn, and fully supported the strict sequestration of L'Estrange's estates.

Of course he was unpopular with Royalists. What about his own side?

Corbet seems to have been regarded as an extremist by the more moderate Parliamentarians. When the army, under Oliver Cromwell, began flexing its muscles and demanding a more radical approach, he was on the side of the radicals. In an expression of raw power in 1648 known as Pride's Purge (named after the army colonel who implemented it) moderate MPs were turned away by force from the Houses of Parliament and only the radicals in favour of putting the king on trial allowed in. Corbet was one of just four

Norfolk members still sitting in what subsequently became known as the Rump Parliament.

What about the king?

By January, 1649, after the outbreak of a second war that involved more terrible suffering and bloodshed in Britain, many were convinced Charles must die. It was a terrifying step to take. As the Lord's anointed many saw the monarch as untouchable. Cromwell and his adherents put him on trial, a famous piece of theatre played out in Westminster Hall. Corbet listed the king's crimes as "the horrid rebellion and bloody massacres of the Protestants in Ireland, the levying of war against the Parliament and the good people in England". The verdict was not in doubt – but there were many who did not dare put their name to the warrant for the king's execution. Miles Corbet was not squeamish; he became the 59th and last signatory.

What happened next?

Corbet went with Cromwell to Ireland, the next place to feel the force of the Puritan army. He became governor of Malahide Castle near Dublin during the 1650s. Lord Protector Oliver Cromwell died in September, 1658. His hapless son Richard inherited the title, but he was nothing like his father. The Commonwealth regime tottered – and soon fell. At the Restoration of the monarchy in 1660 Corbet fled to the Netherlands. The 60 or so surviving regicides – those who had signed the death warrant and been involved in Charles's execution – were put on trial by the new regime of King Charles II, and many executed. In a macabre turn of events, Oliver Cromwell's corpse, buried amid great pageantry less than two years earlier, was exhumed and given over to the full rigours of the law – hanging, drawing and quartering. Eventually Samuel Pepys' boss at the Admiralty, George Downing, lured Corbet and two other regicides into a trap at Delft. They were kidnapped, brought back to England and condemned. Corbet was made of sterner stuff than some who pleaded for their lives. The night before his execution he wrote at length a justification of his actions (quoted in part at the top of this piece) before being hanged, drawn and quartered at Tyburn on April 19, 1662.

Anything else?

According to legend, his ghost still haunts Malahide Castle, appearing in armour before falling apart if anyone meets it.

17th century **1656**

Adventures in the Fens

To anyone travelling through them today, the Fens seem a monotonous landscape. Yet these placid looking, fertile fields have witnessed an elemental struggle between humans and nature. The struggle goes on.

For centuries the land was under water

Before the 17th century this was the Great Eastern Swamp. A vast tract of impenetrable marsh covering parts of Norfolk, Cambridgeshire and Lincolnshire. It was home to a distinctive people, the 'Fen Tigers' who made a precarious living from fishing, waterfowling and reed-cutting. At times it had harboured outlaws, most famously Hereward the Wake who fought the Normans from Ely in the 1070s. To the rest of the country it remained a place apart. From time to time pioneers had tried to improve the land; the Romans built sea walls and causeways, monks who settled on 'islands' such as Ely, Ramsey and Crowland had devised canals and waterways – but the fenland defied them all. While in summer animals could be grazed in the pastures, in winter this land flooded. In 1570 alone high tides led to widespread flooding across East Anglia as far as Bedfordshire. It was a hard place; inhabitants suffered from 'fen ague' – later diagnosed as malaria spread by mosquitoes thriving in stagnant water – and chronic rheumatism. What could be done with such a place?

Leave it in peace?

By the 17th century a growing population needed feeding – and there was money to be made from crop-bearing land. From King Charles I to local landowners, a plan sprang up to produce some 95,000 acres of dry, year-round arable land from the swampy Fens. In 1630, with royal approval, Francis Russell, fourth Earl of Bedford and some 'gentleman adventurers' (think venture capitalists) got together to fund a massive project. They hired a hard-headed, ambitious and uncompromising Dutch engineer named Cornelius Vermuyden to mastermind it. Vermuyden was not afraid to make enemies, which was just as well as he was about to make plenty. Always controversial throughout his career and afterwards, he was to encounter widespread criticism and violent resistance as he undertook a job that took a quarter of a century to complete – and even then it was not the end.

A big job. . .

Vermuyden's bold plan was to straighten the course of existing winding rivers such as the Great Ouse, thus cutting the distance from the sea, and make new cuts to enable water to drain away more effectively. Not everyone agreed, believing drainage improvement by such means as pumping was the answer. In 1631 Vermuyden's army of navigators, many of them Dutch, dug a new river (or 'drain' in Fenland parlance) named The Bedford after his patron. It was a 19-mile long, 70ft wide waterway from Earith to Salter's Lode, near Downham Market. Other work was undertaken at Whittlesey, Wisbech and Crowland. The Fen Tigers resisted all the way; insular and foreigner-hating, they attacked the workers, sometimes armed with scythes and pitchforks, and destroyed the works by night. For a while they enlisted the aid of Ely landowner Oliver Cromwell, who took up their case (he was to change his views a decade later). Understandably, they saw the drainage as an assault on their unique way of life, which would become untenable. As far as they were concerned, these greedy rich men who treated them with such contempt needed stopping. At Wicken there was rioting when both men and stone-throwing women attacked court officials. Nevertheless, by 1637, the work was declared complete.

Right, down tools, plant crops. . .

That winter severe flooding wrecked everything. Many of the adventurers went bankrupt. Many blamed Vermuyden. "Sir Cornelius hath abused the King's Majesty," wrote local man Andrew Bullard, "making hollow and counterfeit banks". Vermuyden hit back in print, his 1642 'Discourse touching the Draining of the Great Fens' defending his record. Nevertheless, it was back to square one. King Charles prepared to invest his own money, intent on founding a royal estate at Manea, near March. The Civil War halted everything, but in 1649 a new Act of Parliament reinstigated the work. Cromwell supported it, Bedford's son financed it and Vermuyden made it happen, despite his critics. This time Scottish and later Dutch prisoners of war did the digging; again, the locals sabotaged their efforts, and again it was eventually completed. This time a 'New Bedford' River was dug parallel to the old. Eventually it was renamed the Hundred Foot Drain after its width. Between the rivers the Ouse Washes, a 4,700-acre storage reservoir hemmed in by enormous banks, was created to hold flood water until it was safe to be released. The Forty Foot was also dug north of Chatteris. The belt on the buckle was at Denver. Vermuyden built a sluice to prevent salt water getting in from the tidal river. People using the river to transport goods were outraged, as the sluice got in the way of speedy navigation, but the Adventurers prevailed. Money talks. By 1656 Vermuyden again declared the work done, and retired to comfortable obscurity. Soon bumper crops of flax, hemp, corn, onions, wheat, woad and peas were being produced.

Hurrah! Happy days . . .

Er . . . not quite. Within a decade or so the water returned with a vengeance. In 1713 high tides flooded the region yet again and destroyed Denver Sluice; it was not rebuilt for 35 years. There was another problem. The drained peat soil shrank alarmingly rapidly, by several feet in places, creating a crazy upside down world in which rivers are higher than the surrounding countryside. Windmills powering drainage machinery became a common sight, while in the 19th century steam-powered pumps arrived to ease the burden. The drained Fens eventually realised the dreams of Cornelius Vermuyden and the Adventurers, and today the area produces an abundance of crops – but by nature this land really ought to be under water. Flooding remains a threat when high tides and bad weather combine, as we saw to devastating effect in 1947 and 1953. In recent wet winters the washes at Welney have been under water, impassable to traffic for weeks at a time. Our favourite traffic sign was one spotted a few years ago on the B1094 road between Nordelph and Welney, which declared, rather nonchalantly, "Road closed due to flooding. Find your own route". If sea levels rise, as predicted due to global warming, the Fens will be affected. Constant vigilance is the key. Although 1656 was a significant year, changing the history and nature of the Fens, this story is far from over. Nature has a funny habit of winning in the end.

17th century **1688**

The indomitable Dean

"We are here at a miserable passe with this horrid sot we have got for our Dean. He cannot sleep at night till dosed with drink. . ."

A harsh assessment

Humphrey Prideaux, cleric, scholar and author, had a rough tongue and a rougher pen. The above is his censorious opinion of his predecessor as Dean of Norwich, and wholly typical of the unclerical language he frequently used about those who failed to live up to his standards. Nevertheless, he was a tireless administrator for the cathedral he grew to love over the space of 40 years, and a man who overcame great personal pain to do the one job he always coveted.

Easier to admire than to like. . .

He was born in 1648 in Padstow, Cornwall. Destined from youth for the Church, he attended Christ Church College, Oxford, becoming a Master of Arts in 1675. An awkward character, he did not seek out friends. His biggest influences were two older men; the college Dean Dr John Fell and Orientalist scholar Dr Edward Pococke. His series of letters to former colleague and friend John Ellis illustrate his poor opinion of fellow students. Many were "dunces and knaves", while Balliol College was a "dingy, horrid scandalous alehouse". His view of Oxford was not to improve with the years, though he remained a tutor there until the 1680s.

How did he end up in Norwich?

In 1681 he became a prebendary at Norwich Cathedral. The city, then the second largest in the country, made an immediate impact on Prideaux. He later described Norfolk as the "pleasantest country in England, being all open and dry". In the enclosed world of the Cathedral Close, he was in his element, and was able to settle permanently in the county by 1685. He married the following year, his bride being a squire's daughter, Bridget Bokenham, from Suffolk. Although this began as a marriage of convenience, he later gave his wife and children as much affection as he could. Prideaux became the vicar of Saham Toney, near Watton, but had little time to devote to it. The mid-1680s were momentous times in Britain. The new King James II was an open Roman Catholic, and this spelled trouble for all Church of England clergymen. Ever since the Reformation of the 1530s Britain had been split by religious dissent. The outcome of the civil wars of the 1640s and eventual restoration of the monarchy in 1660 had seemed to spell the end of this disharmony. The Church of England was the established religion of the country. All other denominations – from Catholics to Protestant dissenters such as the Quakers – were largely excluded from power. By the late 1680s things were in flux once again. Norwich was not as badly affected as other regions. "We live here remote from the centre of affairs and in a great deal of quiet," wrote Prideaux early in 1688. That was all to change.

The Glorious Revolution?

Historians, like all of us, are often wise after the event, and sometimes regard the fall of James II as somehow inevitable. It was not. To oppose the king in 1688 was to court imprisonment, or worse. In 1685 the Duke of Monmouth, an illegitimate Protestant son of Charles II, landed in the west country intent on deposing his Catholic uncle. He raised an army, but it was crushed by the king's army at Sedgemoor in Somerset. Monmouth was beheaded, and many of his supporters lost their lives both in battle and subsequently at the so-called 'Bloody Assizes'. When James proposed a Declaration of Indulgence for Catholics and other dissenters from the Church of England, what seemed on the surface like a liberal act was interpreted as an assault on Protestantism. The Anglican bishops, including Prideaux's superior at Norwich, William Lloyd, refused to accept this, and seven of them were sent to the Tower of London. Prideaux unswervingly supported the bishops to the extent of distributing two thousand copies of a letter sent by them to Anglican clergy urging them not to read the Declaration in their churches. This was later seen as influential in weakening the authority of the king, who fell later in November of that year after the landing in the west country of William of Orange from the Netherlands. James was this time deserted by his army, and fled into exile. Protestant mobs in Norwich attacked known or suspected Catholics; Prideaux protected those living in the Close by locking the gates to stop the looters. It was a rare example of him getting involved in the affairs of the city, with which he was careful not to meddle.

What happened after the Revolution?

He was able to keep his living, and also swear allegiance to the new king and queen, William and Mary. But he now had problems closer to home. The newly appointed Dean of Norwich was the hard-drinking Dr Henry Fairfax, mentioned at the top of this story. The two quickly fell out, with Prideaux roundly denouncing Fairfax's conduct. Prideaux became so obsessed with the Dean's alleged misconduct, he withdrew from Norwich and lived in Saham Toney for the best part of five years. Nor did he get on with the new bishop, John Moore, who was appointed in 1691.

Perhaps he needed to work on his people skills?

That's not the way he saw it. Earlier in his career he wrote: "There is nothing which I doe so much desire. . . as to be fixed in a station once for all where I may have as little trouble as possible." In 1702 he got his wish. Fairfax died, and Prideaux became Dean, the role he always wanted. He set about reform. The cathedral building, which had been in a state of disrepair since the destruction wrought during the religious upheaval of the Civil War, was strengthened; the Dean's work on the steeple was credited with ensuring it survived the Great Storm of 1703. He also kept a close eye on the Close and its tenants, making sure undesirables were sent packing and everyone behaved themselves. If he was content in his work, Prideaux's private life was less happy. In 1700 he was grief-stricken when his wife died, and the remaining 24 years of his life were dominated by ill health. For many years he suffered from a stone in his bladder, an agonising complaint which may have accounted for some of his bad temper. Following a risky operation in 1711 he was left an invalid.

Did he have to give up his job?

Not likely. His mind was as sharp as ever, and he maintained his reign until his death in 1724. Prideaux's fame was established for contemporaries by two major historical books which reflected his early learning at Oxford; Life of Mahomet (1697), and The Old and New Testament Connected in the History of the Jews and Neighbouring Nations (1715-17) of which many editions were published.

18th century **1707**

Sir Cloudesley's curse

Let his children be fatherless and his wife a widow

This curse comes from Psalm 109 – and is relevant to the tragic story of Sir Cloudesley Shovell.

Big wig: Sir Cloudesley Shovell came to an untimely end.

The name sounds comical

Well, the man wasn't. He was, at the time of his death, the Lord High Admiral of England, a renowned fighting sailor and a man with a hot temper you would have been advised not to risk provoking by making fun of his name. Shovell, whose name was probably pronounced 'Show-el', was born at Cockthorpe, near Holt, in November, 1650, of a distinguished if not wealthy county family. One of those Norfolk men with 'one foot on land and one in the sea' he was destined for the Navy. Along with fellow Norfolk sailors Sir Christopher Myngs and Sir John Narborough, he was in the thick of things in the Mediterranean. At this time the Royal Navy was beginning to become a force outside its home waters, expanding into the Mediterranean and getting involved in a series of wars largely involving protecting the country's trade and harming that of its rivals. Young Cloudesley, whose unusual Christian name came from a maternal grandmother's surname, first went to sea aged 12 or 13. Like Horatio Nelson a century later, he was a cabin boy under the command of a relative, Sir Christopher Myngs. During the Anglo-Dutch War of 1672 he was a midshipman aboard the Duke of York's flagship, HMS Royal Prince. He saw action in the Battle of Sole Bay, fought off Southwold. Shovell proved himself a brave and able seaman; in 1674 he attacked and destroyed four pirate ships under the walls of Tripoli, the stronghold of the fearsome Barbary corsairs, who had raided throughout Europe, including the shores of western Britain and Ireland, in search of loot and slaves to be sold in North Africa.

Didn't the Navy usually fight the French?

Apart from a brief spat in the 1620s Britain and France had been – uncharacteristically – at peace for more than a century until William of Orange became king after the 'Glorious Revolution' of 1688. This put the country on a collision course with the powerful France of 'Sun King' Louis XIV, William's sworn enemy. Normal service was resumed. Britain would be at war with France and its allies, with an interval of only a few years, from 1690 until 1714. Shovell was again to the fore. Now a rear-admiral, he fought at the battles of Beachy Head, off Ireland, and La Hogue (1692), helping to defeat a French fleet en route to escorting troops bound for an invasion of Britain. Shovell made himself and his crews rich by seizing French and Spanish commercial shipping and helped to capture Gibraltar in 1704 during the War of the Spanish Succession. Britain still holds the Rock, that vital sea base, to this day. As commander-in-chief of the British fleet, he aided the Earl of Peterborough in the capture of the port of Barcelona the following year, and attacked Toulon on the southern French coast.

What about that temper?

In October, 1707, his fleet was returning home from the Mediterranean when it ran into one of the worst storms of the century off the Scilly Isles. Neither the admiral nor his navigators knew exactly where they were, in the "dirty weather". They thought – or hoped – they were safely west of Ile d'Ouessant, an island off Brittany. Instead, they found themselves in dangerous waters around the Scilly Islands. According to a popular legend, which seems to have grown with the telling, one of the sailors aboard his flagship, The Association, was a local man who knew the waters well. He rushed to warn the admiral that the ships were heading towards dangerous Gilstone Reef. Far from thanking the man for his advice, Shovell ordered him hanged.

Harsh – and not very fair

The Navy was not a democracy – and admirals did not take kindly to common sailors telling them how to sail their ships. Merely keeping an independent navigation log, as this crewman did, was considered an act of mutiny. Orders were to be obeyed without question, but Sir Cloudesley's action seems an overreaction. As the poor sailor was strung up, he recited the curse from Psalm 109 as retribution against the admiral. Many modern naval historians have poured scorn on this story; it has entered legend, but no witnesses survived to bear testament, so we must take it with a pinch of salt. The Association foundered on the rocks. She sank quickly, going down with all hands. The Eagle and Romney also struck the rocks and sank. Four warships perished that day – October 22, 1707. Two thousand men lost their lives. Among them were the admiral's two stepsons, from his marriage to Lady Elizabeth Narborough, widow of his former commanding officer and fellow Norfolk man, Sir John. Shovell's body was washed ashore at Porthellick Cove, on the island of St Mary's in the Scilly Isles. He was taken back to England and buried in Westminster Abbey. Some thirty years later, though, an elderly local woman made a macabre deathbed confession. A well-known 'wrecker' of ships that came to grief on the treacherous shores, she said she had found the admiral alive but, seeing he had many rings on his fingers including one fine sapphire, she hacked them off and buried him – alive – on the beach. That sailor's curse had some power. This is another rather colourful story doubted by historians – but is too good not to be told!

How did the fleet come to be in the wrong place?

Sir Cloudesley was a fine navigator, but he and his crew were handicapped by the inability to accurately read longitude. Sailors of the day could place a ship's position by latitude, but the secrets of longitude eluded them. Many died as a result. It was the death of the celebrated admiral which led to prize money being put up for the person who devised a way of solving the problem. In the end it was Yorkshire clockmaker Thomas Harrison's sea clock that won it – his struggle to get the invention accepted is told in Dava Sobel's acclaimed book Longitude.

Anything else we should know about Sir Cloudesley?

He was also a fashion guru. It is said he invented the hairpiece that gave rise to the term 'big wig'.

Admiral 'Old Grog'

'Old Grog'? He's named after a drink?

Grog is indeed an old-fashioned term for alcohol, popular with the Armed Forces. Admiral Edward Vernon gave the Royal Navy rum ration its distinctive name. This colourful and popular 18th century sailor, who later became MP for Ipswich, distinguished himself in Caribbean waters, but his fiery nature saw him fall out with the Admiralty. To this day, his name is renowned in Jamaica, the USA – and a Suffolk pub he is said to haunt.

He liked a tipple then?

Abstainers were pretty rare in the Royal Navy of the 1700s. It is fair to assume Vernon was not one to buck the trend – within limits. He certainly didn't want his men to drink too much, as we will see. He was born at Westminster in 1684, the son of James Vernon, a secretary of state under King William and Queen Mary. After education in London and Oxford he went to sea, aged 16. With war being waged against France and Spain the young man had every chance of making a name for himself. He served with Norfolk's Admiral Sir Cloudesley Shovell at the Battle of Malaga in 1704, and was present at the capture of Gibraltar from Spain that year. Having served aboard HMS Ipswich from 1701, still aged only 24, he became captain of HMS Jersey – and sailed for Jamaica and the Spanish Main. His arrival in the West Indies marked the beginning of a long and fruitful association with the island of Jamaica.

He wasn't there for a holiday!

The Caribbean was a theatre of war for the competing colonial powers in the region; England, France and Spain. Islands such as Jamaica and Antigua were the headquarters of a mighty English fleet. Vernon returned to Jamaica several times during his career, serving as Commodore of Port Royal during the 1720s. By this time peace had broken out between the powers – but naval and commercial interests at home and in the colonies were urging aggression. In Britain Prime Minister Robert Walpole was for peace and stability; ambitious naval men on the ground like Edward Vernon wanted war against the seemingly weak Spanish empire, which everyone assumed was there for the taking. This was the so-called 'Blue Water' strategy urged by those who wanted war at sea. Fortune and glory beckoned.

Eventually they got their way

In 1731 English merchant captain Robert Jenkins's sloop was boarded by Spanish customs officers in the West Indies and accused of smuggling. He later claimed he had been tortured and had his ear torn off – which he later produced to a stunned House of Commons in London. It was the spark that pushed Walpole into war in 1739; hence the 'War of Jenkins' Ear'. Vernon, now a vice-admiral commanding the whole Caribbean fleet, had his chance. He immediately seized Puerto Bello, Panama. When the news reached London the admiral became an instant hero. More commemorative medals were struck for Vernon than anyone else in the 18th century; pubs were named after him, and London's Portobello Road and Dublin's Portobello took their names from his Panamanian prize. Thomas Arne composed the stirring anthem Rule Britannia in his honour. In Jamaica he was scarcely less popular; on his return "Jamaican ladies swooned and lads hurrahed and tossed their caps". Vernon's descendants were to stay on the island for several generations. He next took Fort Chagres, on the Isthmus of Darien. The crowning glory was to be an assault on Cartagena, the jewel in the crown of Spain's South American empire. But Vernon's 23,000 strong expedition, hit hard by debilitating tropical disease, was repulsed by a Spanish garrison of just 3,000; lack of co-operation between army and navy was blamed. Few thought less of Vernon though. By 1745 he was promoted to an admiral of the white, second only to admiral of the fleet in the hierarchy of the Royal Navy.

What about that nickname?

In 1740 Vernon grew tired of the drunken behaviour of many of the men under his command. He ordered his sailors' neat rum ration be diluted with water and served out in halves (half at noon, half at sunset). The name stuck as he was already known as 'Old Grog' on account of the grogam coat he wore. Grogam is a coarse fabric of silk mixed with wool or mohair and often stiffened with gum. Versions of the drink included lemon and lime juice, cinnamon or sugar to improve the taste – as well as ensuring the tars got their vitamins to ward off diseases such as scurvy, then the scourge of the Navy. Serving 'grog' sped through the British and American fleets; the Royal Navy only ended the tradition in 1971. The admiral's concern for his men's welfare is further illustrated by his founding of a hospital in Kingston, Jamaica. Vernon was immortalised by an account produced by novelist Tobias George Smollett, who served as a surgeon's mate during the Cartagena campaign. He wrote up his experiences in his History of England. Commanding the marine contingent was Lawrence Washington, from the then British colonies in America. He was the elder half-brother of George, later commander of the rebel forces who broke away from Britain after 1776 and subsequently the first President of the independent USA. A great friend of the admiral, Lawrence later named his American estate Mount Vernon.

Anything else?

Although lauded by the public, the feisty Vernon didn't always get on well with the authorities. Several Jamaican governors resented his high-handedness; one accused him of smuggling, while he almost fought a duel with another. This he could survive, but arguing with the Admiralty in London was another matter entirely. In 1746, while in charge of guarding the south coast of England, he was struck from the list of admirals for insubordination. His naval career, which had spanned nearly half a century, was at an end. By this time he had found another outlet – politics. In 1741 he was elected MP for Ipswich, and sat for the town in Parliament for more than a decade, where he was a harsh critic of the government on naval matters. He died at his home at Nacton, Suffolk, in 1757.

His spirit lives on, and not just the rum. . .

Old Grog's ghost has been spotted in two places. In Jamaica he is said to have been seen when the rays of the full moon glance off the waters of Kingston harbour. Closer to home, Ipswich's Evening Star newspaper reported a few years ago that a psychic saw the admiral's shade in the Woolpack pub, Tuddenham Road, Ipswich. The Admiral Vernon pub at Over, near Cambridge, is named after him. Appropriate for a man best remembered today for an alcoholic drink.

18th century **1748**

Portraits of an age

In 1748 a young artist began work on a portrait of a wealthy newly wed couple. The painter was Thomas Gainsborough, the couple were Robert and Frances Andrews. But the real star of the show is the East Anglian countryside.

Local boy made good?

Thomas Gainsborough was the son of a Sudbury wheeler-dealer who made it to the heart of Britain's art establishment. The faces from more than 200 years ago stare back at us. Lifelike and characterful beneath the wigs and finery, they look perhaps more confidently than we can towards the future, sure of their place in society. But there was more to Gainsborough too than met the eye. According to Mark Bills, director of Sudbury's Gainsborough House, the artist "was someone you would like to meet". While you could admire his artistic rivals, such as Sir Joshua Reynolds, "Gainsborough was an artist you could love". Today the town house where the painter was born in 1727, and where he passed his early years before the bright lights of London called, is a museum dedicated to his life. You can see many of the artist's works at the museum, which has been open since 1961. Because Gainsborough was so rooted in his native land, his work was natural and intuitive. Like Suffolk's John Constable, a later admirer of his work, his landscapes were snapshots of their time. He was most at home with country scenes – the now iconic painting of Mr and Mrs Andrews, held today by the National Gallery in London, showing the Stour valley from the Auberies estate overlooking Sudbury, is his best known – but he made his money and contemporary fame from the lucrative business of portrait painting for wealthy clients.

But his native landscape was his real love

He grew tired of portrait painting – "the curs'd face business" – preferring the natural world. "Nature was his teacher and the woods of Suffolk his academy," wrote one biographer after Gainsborough's death in 1788. As Constable himself put it: "The landscape of Gainsborough is soothing, tender and affecting. . . on looking at them we find tears in our eyes, and know not what brings them on." In 1722 weaver and businessman John Gainsborough bought "a most excellent Brickt Mansion" in Sudbury on a plot that had been inhabited since medieval times. Five years later his fifth son, and ninth child, Thomas, joined the growing family. They knew both good times and bad as John's economic fortunes fluctuated. Thomas showed artistic promise. Aged 13 he was apprenticed to a London silversmith, where he learnt such skills as engraving. Later he studied art at St Martin's Lane Academy. Contemporaries included such artists as William Hogarth, and no doubt young Thomas learnt a great deal at the heart of Britain's artistic and economic metropolis.

Time to make his way in the world

By the time his father died in 1748, Thomas was married – to Margaret Burr, an illegitimate daughter of the Earl of Beaufort. The young couple lived in Sudbury for the next three years, before the need to make more money from portrait painting led them to rent a property in Foundation Street, Ipswich. There they lived for a further seven years, when a move to Bath propelled them into the orbit of the great and good of Georgian society. Eventually, Gainsborough moved to London where the family lived in a large property in Pall Mall. As a founding member of the Royal Academy he engaged in a long running spat with his rival Sir Joshua Reynolds – though the two made it up before they died. Gainsborough House displays many of Gainsborough's portraits and landscapes. Each of the rooms in the house takes a theme around his life and art. These include a brilliant picture of Mrs Thomas Cobbold and her daughter – of the famous Suffolk brewing family, and his copy of Peter Paul Rubens' Descent from the Cross. Gainsborough is credited with inventing English landscape painting. He was greatly influenced by Dutch masters, particularly Jan van Eyck. In turn he influenced a new generation of Englishmen – such as Constable and the artists of the Norwich School, including John Sell Cotman and John Crome. In later years Gainsborough became a 'celebrity' artist. His subjects included the renowned Georgiana, Duchess of Devonshire, as well as King George III and Queen Charlotte. Gainsborough became the royal family's favourite artist in his later years.

What about Mr and Mrs Andrews?

Gainsborough liked to place his sitters in attractive landscapes – a way of killing two birds with one stone perhaps. He could paint the landscape he loved, while making money from creating the portraits of his wealthy customers. Robert Andrews was a rich landowner, only a little older than Thomas himself. His estate was called the Auberies, at Bulmer Tye in north Essex, four miles from Sudbury, where he had been at school. In November, 1748, he married 16-year-old Frances Mary Carter, and the two set up home. Although members of the landed gentry, both families had made their money from trade, as so many did in the 18th century. The oil on canvas painting measures 69cms in height by 119cms width. This is much smaller than Gainsborough's later full length portraits. You can see All Saints' Church, Sudbury, where the Andrews were married, in the distance. The well-maintained farmland around them belonged to Mr Andrews. The couple went on to have nine children, but Frances died, aged 48, in 1780. Her husband remarried, and lived to the age of 80. This portrait stayed in the Andrews family for two centuries until it was sold for £130,000 at Sotheby's in London. It was little known until an exhibition at Ipswich in 1927 gained it iconic status. Today it is Gainsborough's best known work, and often used in books and other media to illustrate the landed gentry and their society of the mid-18th century.

Did he make any enemies?

Although fiercely loyal to his friends, the artist often fell out with picky clients, and wasn't overly keen on the law and its practitioners. When a Colchester lawyer who had sat for a portrait wanted changes made, Gainsborough wrote back that he was sorry he did not realise he was a lawyer for he had far too honest a face! On another occasion he gave evidence in a court dispute over whether a painting attributed to the French artist Poussin was authentic. Gainsborough said it was a fake. When an attorney questioned this judgment, he said he felt "the eye of a painter to be the equal to the tongue of a lawyer".

Thomas Gainsborough died of cancer in 1788, and is buried in Kew, Surrey.
Gainsborough House, 46 Gainsborough Street Sudbury, Suffolk C010 2EU
Tel: 01787 372958 mail@gainsborough.org. Open Mon-Sat, 10am-5pm.
The portrait of Mr and Mrs Andrews is at The National Gallery, London.
www.nationalgallery.org.uk/

18th century **1778**

An eccentric Walpole

Another Walpole! Did he become Prime Minister?
George Walpole, Earl of Orford, was a profligate 'rake', country sportsman and all-round Norfolk eccentric. Inheriting a title, great house and enormous prestige, along with debts of £40,000, from his grandfather wasn't enough for George. Over the next 40 years he managed to more than double his debts, and in 1778 he sold off his family's greatest treasures to meet them. In an age of outstanding profligacy and eccentricity among the aristocracy, he is worthy of mention.

Fine performance. How did he do it?
George was born in 1730. His father Robert was the eldest son of political heavyweight Robert Walpole, effective ruler of Britain from 1721 to 1742 and widely regarded as our first prime minister. George's mother was a West Country heiress, Margaret Rolle, who wed Robert at the age of 16 in a disastrous marriage of convenience. After George – named after the reigning Hanoverian monarch – was born in 1730 the couple broke up; Margaret scandalously eloped with her lover to Italy.

Young George grew up without a mother. How did he react?
He seems to have been an affable but unreliable lad. His uncle Horace, who he was to exasperate for the next 50 years, said of his 12-year-old nephew in 1742, he was "a most charming boy, but grown excessively like his mother in the face". Horace, only 13 years older than George, resolved to do his best for this boy from a broken home. Not that he was under-privileged; he would have basked in his grandfather's celebrity at Houghton Hall, the Walpoles' north Norfolk Palladian mansion, where the chief movers in the government gathered, and the royal family paid visits. Work began on Houghton in the 1720s, going on well into the next decade. It reflected Sir Robert's wealth, power and artistic taste. To this end he accumulated an imposing collection of well over 400 Old Master paintings. They included works by Van Dyck, Poussin, Rubens, Rembrandt and Velazquez, as well as a number of Roman

busts. This was George's family background. But his parents' experience of marriage might have put him off the institution; when he came of age he rejected the heiresses his family suggested for a bride. Instead he set up home with Patty Turk, originally a housemaid at Houghton; the two became devoted to each other. Not for the first time his uncle was torn between annoyance and affection. "It is impossible not to love him when one sees him: impossible to esteem him when one thinks on him," he wrote to a friend. In 1751 George's father died, and he inherited the title Earl of Orford, originally bestowed on his grandfather.

And the whole of Norfolk became his playground?

Orford showed no interest in politics, rarely attending the House of Lords and never speaking there. Instead he devoted himself to the country life he adored. Greyhounds and racehorses filled his stables, he bought falcons and surrounded himself with a fast-living set of friends. Uncle Horace denounced them as hangers-on, "a rookery of harpies", but Orford was unabashed. The money kept pouring out, and his eccentricity grew. He fitted out a carriage (known as a phaeton) drawn by four red deer. On one occasion they were chased by hounds from a nearby hunt, careering through the streets of Newmarket before reaching the safety of an inn, where the doors were barred. Orford established Swaffham Coursing Club in 1776 for greyhounds as well as a Falconers' Society. He wasn't a complete playboy though. He maintained his family's traditions and obligations. The Walpoles dominated politics in Norfolk, monopolising parliamentary seats at Castle Rising and King's Lynn. In 1768 Orford persuaded a reluctant but dutiful uncle Horace to stand for the turbulent borough of Lynn. As Lord Lieutenant of the county, in 1759 during the Seven Years' War, Orford raised a militia. He marched them to Hyde Park in London, where they were reviewed by the king. Twenty years later, as fears of a fresh French invasion loomed, he again took over the militia – and ordered the suburbs of Norwich be burned if the French landed on the east coast. He was persuaded to stand down, but insisted on handing out gifts of onions to his officers. By that time, his eccentricity had taken a new turn. In 1773 he was diagnosed insane.

We could see it coming

It was left to his long-estranged uncle to save the day. Horrified by the state of Houghton, Horace took over his nephew's affairs, selling off many of the hounds and horses to pay the bills. Orford made a less than convincing recovery. He promptly re-filled the stables and went on his merry way. The following summer he and Patty, accompanied by an enthusiastic entourage, made a celebrated river trip through the Fens. Starting from the house they rented at Eriswell, near Brandon, (Houghton was expensive to maintain) they sailed along the Little Ouse, through Salter's Lode into the Nene and thence to Whittlesey Mere via Upwell, Outwell and March. Admiring crowds gathered to see them. At Whittlesey, then a giant lake later drained for farmland in the following century, they were joined by First Lord of the Admiralty Lord Sandwich, and some other nautical types. It was a memorable party. A contemporary observed: "In anything he undertook it was a predominant trait in his character to never do anything by halves".

What about those debts?

In 1778, following another bout of mental illness, Orford sold off his grandfather's famous collection of paintings. The Poussins, Van Dycks and Rembrandts, the pride of Houghton, were bought by Catherine the Great, Tzarina of Russia, for about £45,000, a massive sum. Horace, who had painstakingly catalogued the collection as a young man, was outraged. "A madman excited by rascals!" he raged of his nephew. Nonchalant as ever, Orford hung a giant portrait of Catherine at Houghton (it is still there) and named his best greyhound Tzarina in her honour. To be fair, let's remind ourselves that many of the debts had begun before his tenure.

What did people think of him?

Orford was a much-loved figure in Norfolk, despite – or perhaps because of – his eccentricity, and he returned the compliment. The diarist Parson James Woodforde said he was "universally respected" and he continued to ride and hunt in all weathers into his sixties. But, in December 1791, his beloved Patty died suddenly. Distraught, Orford followed her within weeks. He named his long-suffering uncle Horace as his heir. The Houghton estate was eventually inherited by the 1st Marquess of Cholmondeley, the original Sir Robert's grandson in the female line. It was restored to its former glory soon after the First World War, when the 5th Marquess and his family took up residence. Houghton is open to the public from March to September. Military history fans will enjoy The Soldier Museum. Said to be the world's largest private collection of model soldiers, it was started by the 6th Marquess as a boy.

The first 'Jane Austen'

In 1778 literary London was agog. Who was the author of the latest novel going the rounds, being read by people from many walks of life? It was none other than a young woman originally from King's Lynn, though her identity had to be kept a secret at first.

An earlier version of Jane Austen?

Certainly Frances (Fanny) Burney, born at King's Lynn in 1752, was an early trailblazer for female fiction authors at a time when few women wrote for a living. But her life was very different to Jane Austen's. At one time she moved in the very highest of London literary and royal circles, before changing her life completely by moving to France at the height of the Napoleonic Wars. She was the fourth of six children born to Dr Charles Burney, a fashionable and well-connected music master and historian – "that clever dog" as Dr Samuel Johnson called him – and his wife Esther, herself the granddaughter of a French Protestant Huguenot refugee, who had moved to England to escape religious persecution. In 1760 the family moved from Lynn to London. From an early age Fanny was brought into close friendship with what reads like a 'who's who' of the intellectual elite of the age. Apart from Johnson, the actor-manager David Garrick and playwright Richard Brinsley Sheridan were regular callers to the family home in Poland Street.

And they encouraged her to write?

Indirectly, probably. From the age of 16 Fanny had been keeping her secret journal, which she would maintain for 70 years until her death. Addressed to 'Nobody' – as nobody but herself was meant to read it – it records everything going on around her. "Silent, observant Fanny" was good at drawing written portraits of people. Johnson recognised her talent, addressing her as "you little character-monger", and he remained a lifelong admirer. Following her mother's death her father married the widow of a King's Lynn wine merchant. Her stepmother disapproved of her "scribbling" novels – a young lady was not even meant to read anything so salacious, though most did – but she carried on, encouraged by her father's friend, the reclusive playwright Samuel Crisp. Even so, the publication of her first novel in 1778 seems to have taken everyone by surprise.

An overnight success?

Fanny had been secretly writing her novel Evelina for several years before she had it published anonymously. She was terrified of ridicule, particularly as a female writer. The book – the comic story of a sheltered provincial young woman's entry into fashionable London society – got 'rave reviews'. Leading Whig politician and intellectual heavyweight Edmund Burke stayed up all night reading it, as did the artist Sir Joshua Reynolds. But no-one knew for several months that Fanny had written it. For a time she sat at dinner tables and heard the book praised, while keeping her secret from all but her publishers. When the truth came out she became an instant celebrity, feted by the great and good. This may have been the worst thing that could have happened. The constant social whirl around her left her little time for writing, apart from her journal. She published a second novel in 1782 called Cecilia; or, Memoirs of an Heiress (for which she was paid £250). Many critics rated it higher than her debut book – but she was to write only two other books in the following two decades. She did not progress, as Jane Austen was to do in the next generation.

Why not?

Probably because she took a job in the royal household. Her name had become known to King George III and Queen Charlotte, and she took the post of second keeper of the robes, with a salary of £200 a year, at Windsor. She hated the job – seeing it as a glorified servant's role – but learned to love the king and queen for all their idiosyncrasies. She had to attend the queen's toilet, to take care of her lap-dog and her snuff-box, and to help her senior, Mrs Schwellenberg, in entertaining the king's equerries and visitors at tea. This position as an onlooker meant she recorded the early stages of George III's madness (now diagnosed more properly as illness) in her journal. On one occasion, she was chased by him at Kew Palace – a scene made famous in the film The Madness of King George. Later she saw him try to throttle the Prince of Wales at a family dinner (though, given the problems Georgian kings had with their sons, that probably wasn't so surprising!). But Fanny was unhappy as a courtier. Bullied by Mrs Schwellenberg, pestered by James Boswell (Dr

Johnson's friend) who quoted poetry to her through the gates of the castle, and jilted by a courtier, she became ill. After five years at Windsor she resigned.

Back to writing, then?

Retiring to her father's Chelsea house, she met a group of French emigrés fleeing from the Revolutionary regime. Among them was an artillery officer, Alexander D'Arblay, with whom she fell in love. In 1793, at the age of 41, Fanny married him. With only her royal pension to live on they settled in Surrey, with a son – Alexander – born the next year. The publication of her third novel, Camilla, earned her £1,000 and enabled the young family to ward off financial difficulties. Fanny accompanied her husband when he went back to France in 1801 to take up a government job. This was during a short-lived truce between Britain and Napoleonic France. When war broke out again the following year, they were stranded in France for the next 13 years. She underwent an agonising mastectomy operation in 1811 – without anaesthetic – and recorded it all in her journal. Remarkably, she delayed the operation until her husband was away on business to avoid bothering him! Fanny later returned to England and published another novel, The Wanderer, following the death of her husband and father. This fourth book, with the sub-title of 'Female Difficulties', raised issues of prejudice against foreigners in England, and wasn't so popular with fans who preferred her earlier, light-hearted satirical style. Fanny lived until 1840, and was buried alongside her family in Bath.

Any critics?

Compared to her radical contemporary Mary Wollstonecraft, whose Vindication of the Rights of Woman (1791), was an early blast of feminism, Fanny Burney's published works were conservative in style with a high moral tone. Her journal is more racy, with dashes of humour and some sly digs at certain characters. She was certainly admired in her lifetime and afterwards. Her contemporary and fellow novelist Jane Austen (1775-1817) was influenced by Burney's witty dialogue and stories. Austen created immortal classics that have stood the test of time. They are better known than ever today thanks to film and television dramatisations (and Jane Austen's picture is on the new £10 note), but Fanny Burney led the way – and fully deserves her place in history.

Welcome to the revolution

In the 1790s, as Britain geared up for war with France, the revolution began at the Maids Head in Norwich.

Troubled times

On July 14, 1791, the Norwich Revolution Society enjoyed its finest hour. Its members toasted the second anniversary of the French Revolution and the storming of the Paris Bastille. They put forward their very modern democratic ideas at one of the oldest hostelries in the city – and indeed the country – the Maids Head tavern in Tombland. The history of the Maids Head goes back to medieval times; it hosted the Bishop of Norwich in the 1090s, Edward the 'Black Prince' of Wales in the 14th century and (this is disputed) Queen Elizabeth I in 1578. Perhaps more to the point of this story, in 1549 it was used as a base by both Robert Kett's ill-fated Norfolk rebels and the leaders of the government forces which eventually subdued them. By the late 18th century, unrest was once again in the East Anglian air. Radicals met at the Maids Head and the Bell Hotel, in Orford Place. They demanded a new social order. The government of William Pitt the Younger cracked down on radicals. Such was Norwich's reputation for dissent it was known as the 'Jacobin city' – a reference to the Jacobin extremists of revolutionary France. In 1794, with Britain in a desperate war with the French and fearful of domestic unrest, the Government suspended habeus corpus. This ancient legal right, enshrined from the days of Magna Carta, was an ordinary person's protection against arbitrary arrest. To Norwich liberals its suspension was proof of government corruption. By the mid-1790s it is estimated the various radical societies had more than 2,000 members in the city.

Why was Norwich so radical?

The city was home to many textile workers. Most of them laboured from home, and enjoyed independence not known elsewhere. Norwich's relatively broad electoral franchise meant a larger proportion of people from humble backgrounds had the right to vote for city officials. It led to a politicised population, ever ready to take to the streets to fight for their rights. To the mid-18th century writer Gilbert White it was a "great fractious manufacturing town". In 1740 riots over the price of grain and fish had rocked the city, while in 1766 armed citizens had just about restored order after another bread riot. Also, the city had a long history of religious dissent. Baptists, Quakers and non-conformists had thrived there since the 17th century. Baptist minister Mark Wilks was a convinced radical, and he was not alone. Of course, only a minority of Dissenters were revolutionaries, but their traditions made them receptive to new ideas. Ideas can be dangerous. None more so than those generated by the 1789 French Revolution. Initially it was welcomed by many in Britain as the dawn of a liberal era. Soon though, the violent excesses of the French radicals alienated many people. Politician Edmund Burke led the conservative backlash with his book Reflections on the Revolution in France. But the spark was ignited by a Norfolk man. Thomas Paine, born in Thetford in 1737, published The Rights of Man, partially to rebuff Burke. A clarion call for democracy, it inspired many throughout Britain – and appalled many others for whom democracy meant mob rule. Soon the London Corresponding Society was formed, a body of radicals influenced by Paine, and established links with other societies nationwide.

And in Norwich?

Historian E P Thompson, in his groundbreaking 1963 work The Making of the English Working Class, described Norwich as "by far the most impressive provincial centre". From groups of working people gathering to discuss events, a number of societies mushroomed. They included the Norwich Revolution Society and the Norwich Patriotic Society. Members initially came from different walks of life. Grand patrician families supplied sympathisers from the Quaker Gurneys, bankers and founders of Barclays, plus manufacturer William Taylor, a renowned intellectual who preferred translating German romantic works to commerce. He was known as "Godless Billy" for his views. Soon after the 1789 uprising he visited Paris and returned brimming with enthusiasm for the revolution and its ideals. Most activists were artisans, wage-earners, small masters and tradesmen; self-employed people without an unsympathetic employer who could sack them. These "urban craftsmen with long intellectual traditions" – in Thompson's phrase – were radicalised. As they moved to the left they demanded democracy, an end to monarchy and aristocracy, and opposed the State, war and taxation. At their height the 40 or so societies boasted 2,000 members. They had links with colleagues in Wisbech, King's Lynn and Great Yarmouth. Meeting in places such as The Bell – headquarters of the Revolution Society – and The Weavers Arms, home of the Patriotic Society, this was a grass roots movement. An intellectual journal, The Cabinet, provided a vehicle for radical views.

What was the reaction?

As war broke out in 1793 the government retaliated. The radicals became unpopular, as many saw them as traitors. So-called 'Church and King' mobs harassed known radicals, and many were arrested. As habeus corpus was suspended in May, 1794, radicals from London to Scotland, and Sheffield to Norwich were arrested. Isaac Saint and other Norwich committee members were hauled in. Juries proved reluctant to convict in such political cases. When two London men were acquitted of high treason that October, Norwich delegate Jonathan Davey was at the Old Bailey for the trial. He rode through the night back to Norfolk, and arrived at St Paul's Baptist Chapel as minister Mark Wilks was in the middle of a service. "Praise God from whom all blessings flow," declared Wilks when Davey told him the news. But it did not result in eventual victory for revolutionary ideals. The mood changed, as Britain's fight with first Revolutionary, and then Bonapartist, France became a battle for national survival in the 1790s and early 1800s. With Britain threatened by French invasion, most people rallied to protection of hearth and home. Diehards like Wilks kept their faith, preaching sermons. But when London radical John Thelwall toured East Anglia, things turned ugly. Although Thelwall spoke 22 times in Norwich, at Great Yarmouth he and his audience were attacked by sailors armed with cutlasses and cudgels. The magistrates at Lynn and Wisbech refused him protection.

And back at the Maids Head?

It wasn't all radicals. A month before the 1791 revolutionary dinner, a very different party enjoyed the tavern's hospitality. Parson James Woodforde, vicar of Weston Longville, near Norwich, kept a regular diary for many years. On June 15 he recorded that he and 35 other Church of England clergymen sat down to eat. The Bishop of Norwich chipped in, donating one bottle of wine between every two clergymen (bottles were much smaller then than they are today. . .) The Maids Head continues to thrive as a hotel in the 21st century, while The Bell remains a popular city centre venue.

18th century **1796**

The Norfolks come home

In 1796 a fever-wracked band of soldiers, survivors of a brutal campaign, came home to Norwich. They were the remnants of the 9th Regiment of Foot, whose successors still give their all in the 21st century.

A welcome fit for heroes?

Some 128 officers and men made it back to Norfolk from the Caribbean in 1796. The 9th – known as the East Norfolk Regiment – had won little glory fighting in Tobago, Guadaloupe, Martinique and St Lucia. Their numbers had been whittled down by disease rather than battle against the French. Today, the West Indies are viewed as a tropical paradise, but in the 18th century they were "the white man's graveyard", the posting every soldier dreaded. Yellow fever and malaria were the killers; in St Lucia in 1795 the garrison reported 575 fit men and 625 sick. It was not the first time the Norfolk regiment had been tested to the utmost, nor the first time they proved steadfast.

A long and proud history?

The regiment traces its origins to 1685 when the Duke of Monmouth challenged his uncle, King James II, for the crown. James raised eight new regiments. Colonel Henry Cornwell was one of those who raised about 1,000 infantry; a mix of pikemen and musketeers. Before they were ready to fight, Monmouth was defeated at Sedgemoor, and executed. The regiment marched up and down the country, with little connection to Norfolk. In its first three years, Cornwell's men – regiments were referred to by their colonel's name, and they were not known by a number until 1747 – were stationed in London, Scotland, the west country and on the south coast. The regiment was 'blooded' in action in Ireland. By this time their founder, King James, was the enemy. England's new king, the Dutch Protestant William III, defeated James's Catholic forces at the Boyne in 1690. The men of the 9th could be forgiven divided loyalties in these confusing times.

An elite force?

Commanding officers came and went. Cornwell resigned after a couple of years, and it was not until Col William Stuart took over, in 1715, that continuity was established. Recruitment was a problem. For many in the working class, service in the army was regarded as disgraceful, so the ranks were filled with often reluctant troops, many of whom joined up to avoid prison – or worse – or for the rum ration. A private soldier earned 8d a day, while their colonel got 12s, a major 7s, ensigns 3s, sergeants 1s 6d and corporals and drummers 1s a day. In the absence of regular barracks, soldiers were billeted compulsorily in taverns and private houses. They were not always welcome. Discipline was fierce, with floggings for minor infringements. Despite this the British soldier was renowned for his stoical endurance; the men did their job out of loyalty to their mates and the regiment rather than patriotism or glory. The Duke of Wellington later described his men as "the scum of the earth", and this is how many were treated. A soldier's life was terribly hard.

Probably better off in battle. . .

Pikes were replaced by bayonets late in the 17th century as the science of war changed. The men wore red coats lined with orange, grey breeches and white stockings, and a felt hat turned up on one side. Training focused on musketry and drill. Following a series of battles against France in the Low Countries, the 9th really made their mark as Britain sent an army to Spain. The Battle of Almanza, in April 1707, was a defeat for the British and their Dutch allies against a Franco-Spanish force. But the 9th fought heroically and took heavy casualties. Tradition has it they were granted the right to portray the helmeted image of Britannia as their regimental badge after this date. The story, too good not to be told, goes that the Spanish saw the banners, and mistook Britannia for the Virgin Mary; hence the regiment's nickname, The Holy Boys. Their reputation for steady courage was forged here; they adopted the motto 'Firm', and became known as the kind of troops who could be depended on in a tight spot. Following a long period of home service, the 9th headed west. In 1762 they were at a successful attack on Havana in Cuba. Disease took a far greater toll on the men than battle. An even greater test awaited them in America. During the American War of Independence, they joined Gen John Burgoyne's army, where they fought with what the general called "steadiness and bravery" against terrible odds in a disastrous campaign. In 1777, Burgoyne was comprehensively defeated by the Americans at Saratoga, and the 9th spent the next three miserable years in captivity.

Better was to come

Sent to Norwich in 1780 to recover and recruit, King George III emphasised the regiment's local association for the first time, saying the regiment should "take the county name of 9th or East Norfolk Regiment. . . so as to create a mutual attachment between the county and the regiment which may at all times be useful towards recruiting the regiment". Although they were not to be christened The Norfolk Regiment until 1881, the link got stronger. For the next seven years they were billeted in and around Norwich, settling in to the area. It was not until 1787 that they received the order everyone dreaded – off to the West Indies. From the low point of their return – just 15 officers, 10 sergeants, 14 drummers and 80 rank and file mustering in Norwich in 1796 – the regiment began recruiting locally. From then they were stationed throughout East Anglia, at Great Yarmouth, Ipswich, Colchester, Stowmarket, Bury St Edmunds and Sudbury. A private's daily pay was boosted to a princely 1s (2½d after stoppages). Three years later the 9th could boast three battalions, and were in the front line in Britain's fight against Napoleon.

Success at last?

In 1808 Napoleon invaded Spain and Portugal. Britain, hitherto invincible at sea but less successful on land, saw an opportunity to land an army, resupplied and supported by the Royal Navy, to counter French ambitions, and aid our Portuguese and Spanish allies. It was a long campaign, more than five years of hard slog up and down the Iberian Peninsular. The 9th were there for much of the time, and distinguished themselves at places such as Rolica, Vimeiro, La Corunna, Busaco, Salamanca, Vittoria, St Sebastian and Nive. At La Corunna, northern Spain, they formed part of a backs-to-the-wall rearguard as Sir John Moore's army was evacuated by the Navy. Moore was killed in battle, and the Norfolks "buried him darkly at dead of night". They were the last British soldiers to leave Spain on the ships. The 9th subsequently suffered wretched casualties during the disastrous Walcheren expedition to the Netherlands – where marsh fever killed more men than died in battle. Sent back to Spain, they formed a vital part of the Duke of Wellington's eventually victorious Peninsular army, following him in a successful invasion of southern France. The 9th were posted all over the empire during the 19th century. In 1881 they became the Norfolk Regiment; the Royal title was added in 1935 – but in 1959 they amalgamated with the Suffolk Regiment, and now form part of the Royal Anglians.

19th century **1816**

Crime and punishment

In May, 1816, a riot broke out in Downham Market. Three months later, 16 people were sentenced to death at the Norwich Assizes. Welcome to crime and punishment – 19th century style.

Hanged for stealing a loaf of bread?

In 1810 England and Wales had 222 capital offences on the statute books. Many offences were subdivided; for example there were seven different kinds of arson, so there were about 20 different crimes for which you could be executed. The harshness of the legal code went back a long way. The Elizabethans made it a capital offence to steal from the person, and things became harsher still. In 1723, in response to a crime spree prompted by armed gangs of deer poachers, the notorious Waltham Black Act was passed. It made offences related to poaching, harming livestock and trespass capital offences. In addition to the draconian 1715 Riot Act, it ushered in a number of so-called 'Black Acts' which extended capital punishment. The Riot Act was brought in during a period of political turbulence, which led to riots on the streets. It authorised local officials, such as justices of the peace or sheriffs, to read out the terms of the Act in public towards any group of 12 people or more to be "unlawfully assembled and thus have to disperse or face punitive action". It enabled authorities to use force without fear of any legal consequence. Partially a disincentive to criminals in an age when few offenders were caught, partially an aggressive attitude towards the lower orders, many of whom were seen as dangerous, it was a savage legal system. As the 19th century dawned, and the poor were hit by trade slumps and the effects of the Napoleonic Wars, working people dreaded the law.

With good reason?

The 1816 Downham Market riot had begun as a protest over the low wages paid by local landowners to farmworkers. Earlier that month a similar protest at Soham, near Ely, had ended in violence. When magistrates at Downham's Crown Inn were insulted, the Upwell Yeomanry Cavalry were called out, the

Riot Act read and the mob dispersed. Of the 16 sentenced to death, two were executed; Daniel Harwood and Thomas Thoday. They were hanged on Castle Hill, Norwich, on August 31, 1816. Nevertheless, reform was in the air. From 1800 judges could commute death sentences – and frequently did. Parliamentary reformers such as Sir Samuel Romilly succeeded in removing the death penalty for pickpockets and other relatively minor offenders. By 1823 the Black Acts were largely repealed, and it was harder to find juries willing to convict when they knew an offender faced the death penalty. Nineteen of the 24 Soham rioters initially condemned to death had the sentence commuted – though transportation to Australia must have felt like death to families left behind. Punishment remained fierce.

A grim business. . .

In the first three decades of the century, executions were common for sheep, cattle and horse stealing. Trowse man Thomas Sutton, whose horse-thief father had been executed, swung in 1808 for destroying a barn full of barley. Sutton had 'form', having already been transported for stealing a pony. After he "behaved in a most audacious manner to the judge" he was executed at Castle Hill. The same grim venue saw two young men, John Allen and John Day, hanged in 1801 for burglary, itself a capital offence. While murderers were regarded as getting their just deserts, an offender such as James Balcham, executed in 1808 for theft, drew some sympathy. At his funeral, a sermon was preached to 1,000 people. Many of those executed left families in dire straits; Binham farmer Thomas Moy, for example, left behind a wife and seven young children when he was hanged for sheep-stealing in 1816. Not every thief was executed. Great Ellingham farmer John Smith, who stole a silver spoon from a public house, was transported for seven years in 1816. Forging banknotes was a capital offence, but Robert Lord and John Watson, both convicted at Thetford that year, also had the sentence commuted to transportation.

A public spectacle?

Executions were nasty. Thomas Thoday, the 1816 Downham rioter, was overcome with grief at his execution at leaving behind a wife and children. When was hanged in Norwich in 1816, "he was nearly sinking down under the agony and grief and terror, and was obliged to be supported by several men," a Norfolk Chronicle reporter wrote. When Peter Donahue, a sergeant in the 30th Regiment of Foot, was executed at Lynn for issuing counterfeit notes, the hanging was botched. "He appeared sensible for many minutes. . . and a large effusion of blood gushed from his mouth and nose." Executions drew large crowds, and gave opportunities for more crime and disorder. When, in 1822, two murderers from Wells-next-the-Sea were hanged in Norwich, "not more than three yards from the gallows, a boy was knocked down by a gentleman who detected him picking his pockets". Nevertheless, hangings remained popular, drawing attendances in the thousands for the more notorious criminals. At one execution in 1829 "crowds of women bringing young children" were observed. The sympathy evident for sheep-stealers and rick-burners did not extend to murderers. When, in 1807, Martha Alden was convicted of killing her husband, local people destroyed her house in Attleborough. Following her execution it was rumoured her ghost 'walked' on Castle Hill.

Any light relief?

In 1817 sportsmen "who had long resisted the threats and entreaties of inhabitants at Old Buckenham" were convicted before Larlingford magistrates and fined – for playing cricket on the village green on a Sunday.

Outrageous behaviour! There was little relief for the poor. . .

In the 1820s impoverished farmworkers again protested against landowners. Machine-breaking and rick-burning broke out. Some offenders were executed, among them Peninsular War and Battle of Waterloo army veterans Noah Peak and George Fortis. The two ex-soldiers were hanged in April, 1822 at Norwich for firing straw stacks. "It is not three years since Peak came to Norwich and conveyed home for burial Edward Fisher, his fellow parishioner, who was executed on the Hill in August, 1819 for stabbing William Harrison," wrote a reporter. As the 19th century progressed, the law became a little more liberal. Although the 1830 Swing Riots were harshly punished, subsequently executions became rarer as the number of capital crimes was reduced. In 1861 the civilian death penalty was reduced to five offences; murder, treason, espionage, arson in royal dockyards and piracy with violence. In 1973 the death penalty was abolished for all except treason, and in 1998 done away with altogether. As for the Riot Act, it stayed on the statute books until 1967. The phrase to "read the Riot Act" became shorthand for administering a firm warning, for example from a teacher to unruly students, though it is seen as a little archaic now.

Reform – or revolution

On June 7, 1832, people in King's Lynn and Norwich celebrated. King William IV, against his will, had agreed to an Act of Parliament that probably averted a revolution. And not before time, many would say. . .

You say you want a revolution. . .

Many historians believe the closest Britain ever came to revolution was in 1832. In that year the rising middle classes finally forced the traditional aristocracy into admitting them into the government of Britain, following years of agitation. An extension of the voting franchise widened the electorate and began to clear up some of the dead wood and idiosyncrasy that had characterised the old House of Commons. Reformers wanted to abolish a system where 'rotten boroughs', with a handful of electors controlled by a powerful aristocratic patron, had as many Parliamentary seats as a place like Manchester, with thousands of disenfranchised people. It wasn't just middle class radicals on the warpath. Discontent was reaching dangerous levels among the urban and rural poor. East Anglia was among the regions affected by the Swing Riots in the autumn of 1830, when agricultural workers began breaking machinery and burning hayricks. Insurrection was in the air. Something had to give.

Even in Norfolk?

Norfolk and East Anglia were being left behind by the Industrial Revolution. Nevertheless Norwich, with a relatively broad voting franchise, many of them artisans in the declining weaving trades, had a reputation for holding lively elections. During the 1790s activists in the city had been at the forefront of calls for reform, before war with revolutionary France brought about a conservative backlash. From 1802 to 1830 the city returned MP William Smith to Parliament. He was a radical liberal who favoured reform. The borough of King's Lynn also had an opinionated electorate. Things could get out of hand at election time. In 1822 a mob destroyed Colonel John Walpole's polling booth, stoned the poll clerks, smashed the windows of the Duke's Head inn and tore the Corporation flag to pieces. A detachment of dragoons arrived from Norwich to end the strife, and arrest ringleaders. The rest of the county, rural in nature with few people entitled to vote, tended to return candidates favoured by local magnates. Norwich's reform campaign began in 1816. In that year a public meeting was held at St Andrew's Hall, Norwich, agreeing to send a petition to Westminster "to effect a retrenchment of the public expenditure, and a reform in the House of Commons". Nationally, things were moving faster, as campaigners took direct action to force the government's hand. In 1819 a mass meeting in Manchester got out of hand, the militia were called in and a number of demonstrators were killed at St Peter's Fields. It was dubbed the 'Peterloo Massacre', in an echo of the recent Battle of Waterloo. Agitation grew throughout the 1820s, centring on growing manufacturing centres like Birmingham, Leeds and Manchester. When a reform-minded Whig government, headed by Lord Grey, took power, the pressure was on. Grey's Reform Bill passed the Commons, but reached a stumbling block in the House of Lords. Backed by the new king, William IV, the peers set their faces against reform. Campaigns in favour of reform began nationwide.

Norwich was not left out

In 1831 agitation began in Norwich. Another St Andrew's Hall meeting in January saw resolutions passed in favour of reform. Many of the city's leading citizens were there. That March, the Rt Hon Robert Grant, the new Norwich MP, presented a petition in the Commons signed by 7,000 citizens, while Sir William Ffolkes presented a similar petition from county hundreds. As the year went on, the language got more urgent. At another mass gathering in late September, again at St Andrew's Hall, a petition to the Lords declared: "The tranquillity and happiness of this kingdom depend on the complete passing of this great national measure". The Peers continued to oppose the Bill, sparking national outrage. In Norwich, on October 18, a procession headed by musical bands started from Castle Ditches at 10am. After parading through the city it arrived at St Andrew's Hall at noon. There 5,000 people, presided over by the mayor, heard Norwich Union insurance company chief Thomas Bignold, one of the principal speakers and among the leading citizens of the county, send a direct message to the king. He expressed the "ardent hope that such constitutional measures as may be completely effectual for the attainment of this most important object will be forthwith adopted by His Majesty under the advice and assistance of his Ministers".

Everyone in agreement then?

When have we ever all agreed on anything in this country? Popular unrest elsewhere in the country, including violent riots in Bristol and Nottingham, sparked a reaction. A county meeting at Norwich's Shirehall in November, 1831, presided over by Anthony Hammond called for reform, but also backed the peers and the king. The "Norfolk Declaration" expressed "alarm at the extensive innovations proposed by the late Reform Bill" and supported the Lords for "refusing to concur in so dangerous an experiment". Another "Conservative Reform" called for a settlement "founded on a constitutional basis and manifesting a conciliatory spirit". Grey presented several different Bills, all blocked by the House of Lords. In desperation he threatened to create 50 Whig peers to overwhelm the Tory majority in the upper house and force the issue. He resigned as prime minister and the king sent for the war hero who won at Waterloo, the Tory Duke of Wellington, to try to form a government. The duke was unable to get a majority. The windows of his London home – Apsley House – were broken by a disapproving mob. Stalemate was reached. These were the heady 'May Days' when Britain looked set for revolution, and a threatened run on the banks sparked fears of chaos. At the last moment William relented, and told the peers to allow the Bill to pass. It did so on June 7.

Popular move?

With some dissenting voices, the passing of the Bill was welcomed in Norfolk. At Lynn it was met "with great rejoicing". Norwich delayed its celebrations until the following month. "A procession of about 2,400 persons, decorated with blue and white favours, marched from Castle Ditches to the Cricket Ground." It was led by Mr R H Gurney, of the famous Norwich banking family. A total of 2,000 people sat down for dinner in a specially constructed marquee. By contrast, some 200,000 people turned out in Birmingham to mark the moment, a reflection on the changing centres of power and population. It was not democracy. Not yet. The voting franchise was only marginally increased, while working class men and all women were ignored. A further reform act in 1867 widened the franchise, and some working men got the vote as a result. For women, the fight was only just beginning. Not until the early years of the 20th century would universal adult suffrage be achieved. But, for those who prefer evolution to revolution, what happened in 1832 was some sort of progress, and certainly better than barricades and bloodshed.

19th century **1833**

Cricket, lovely cricket

In 1833 a young Norfolk sportsman was the toast of the land. Fuller Pilch's exploits made him one of the heroes of the early years of cricket.

National institution, wasn't it?

Cricket was still in its infancy as an organised sport. The origins of the game are hazy. Like football, it seems to have begun as a country pastime for the common folk. Archive material is scarce, but the game may have been played in Norfolk, as it was throughout southern Britain, by the 17th century. Its first recorded mention comes in a 1745 Norwich Mercury advertisement calling on cricketers to subscribe for the new season. Matches were played between Norfolk and Suffolk from 1764 onwards. By that time the game in the south had been adopted by enthusiastic gentlemen and aristocrats. By the early 19th century the MCC had been formed, and were playing at Lord's. Rules of the game were being laid down.

Who was Fuller Pilch?

He was born in 1804. One recent historian of the early years of cricket, former Prime Minister John Major, says his birthplace was at Brinton, three miles from Holt, though some sources says he was born at Horningtoft. No matter. Holt was the centre for Norfolk cricket. Fuller was the son of tailor Nathaniel Pilch and his wife Frances, the third of cricketing brothers. His siblings Nathaniel and William were fine sportsmen, but Fuller surpassed them. He made his debut, aged 17, in a celebrated match at Lord's alongside his brothers. The Holt team represented Norfolk. Then set in rural land north of London, the home of the MCC was becoming the headquarters of cricket. This match entered folklore, as the celebrated MCC batsman William Ward scored 278 runs over two days. Although Norfolk was not such a strong side as those in the south, Fuller Pilch began to make a name for himself.

Gentleman or player?

Cricket mirrored the hierarchical society of the time in its division between professionals and amateurs. These distinctions were so entrenched they were only abolished in the 1960s. Pilch was a 'player', a man who had to earn his living. For a while he mixed making a wage from cricket with following his father's tailoring trade. He became renowned for his batting, though he was an all-rounder. Over six feet tall, he was a stylish batsman, "long-legged and elegant" wearing, like most players at the time, a top hat. Writing in the 1860s, sporting biographer Arthur Haygarth reckoned him "the best batsman that has ever yet appeared". He invented a new shot – 'Pilch's poke' – characteristic of his forward play. His long reach allowed him to defend by reaching forward and smothering the ball. He was hard to dislodge. Newspapers dubbed him a "merciless tyrant" to bowlers. With first class teams few and far between players like Pilch had to travel in search of a game. In 1827 he starred for the Players against the Gentlemen of Sussex, and against Yorkshire.

What about Norfolk?

Norfolk County Cricket Club was founded in 1827 at Bracondale. Pilch was back in his native county two years later, managing the ground as well as a nearby pub. He also played for Norfolk against the MCC. In 1834 he scored 153 not out against the Yorkshiremen in the north. He piled up the runs, notching 87 and 73 against Yorkshire and 105 not out against Sussex. The game was becoming increasingly popular. Large crowds watched the matches, vast sums were wagered, and cricket was making the headlines. The 1834 match between Norfolk and Yorkshire was headlined by the Norfolk Chronicle as "The Great Match of Cricket" featuring the three Pilch brothers. At that time there was a fashion for 'single wicket' games – straight duels between two players. In June, 1833, he took on a famous Yorkshire player, Thomas Marsden, for the 'Championship of England'. Pilch won in two games at Norwich and Sheffield. Most villages could field a side. When Ashwelthorpe beat Mulbarton in June, 1811, they won 22 bottles of cider and 22lbs of cherries. The game seemed to run in other families, as well as the Pilch brothers. In June, 1825, a match at Litcham featured "six Alexanders of Hingham and the five Cushions of Shipdham, on the one side, against the town of Litcham on the other". Reputations were being forged, and teams were beginning to travel long distances in search of opponents. As stakes were high, presumably this could cover their costs. In 1818 a match at Newmarket Heath between Holt and Newmarket clubs was for 330 guineas a side, while bets "to the amount of several thousand pounds" exchanged hands when Holt played Nottingham four years later. With that kind of money involved, some questionable practices crept in. In August, 1819 a Holt side including Fuller Pilch travelled to Bungay for a match on the Common. It seems the Suffolk side "smuggled" in a couple of professionals from Marylebone. "Much wrangling took place, when Holt refused to go on with the game, and the match was claimed by Bungay," reported the Norfolk Annals. Although a return game was played at Holt, the Norfolk club made a public announcement, "declaring their determination to decline any further contest with the Bungay club". Other matches were more friendly; in 1823 11 married and 11 single women played a match at Hockwold-cum-Wilton for 11 pairs of gloves. The married women won. "The parties were dressed in jackets and trousers tastefully decorated with blue ribbands." The summer game transcended the seasons; a crowd of 1,500 people watched a match played on ice at Diss Mere in February, 1827. This feat was repeated 14 years later when Scoulton Mere hosted a Boxing Day cricket on ice match between two selected elevens from the parish of Hingham, captained by Mr W Waller and Mr W Roberts respectively. "Some of the players wore skates and others their stump shoes to prevent falling."

How was Fuller Pilch progressing?

In 1835 the men of Kent offered him £100 a year to play for them and manage their ground. Kent had a strong eleven, and Pilch's career continued to thrive. In 229 first class matches he scored more than 13,000 runs, including ten centuries. At a time when pitches were little better than meadows, scores were far lower than they are today, so this was quite a feat. John Major describes him as "one of three great cricketers in the second quarter of the 19th century". In the 1840s he joined an itinerant All-England XI led by a Nottinghamshire entrepreneur, William Clarke. This early version of a 'travelling circus' proved popular, playing to packed houses around the land. Pilch, "easy-natured and popular", was among the stars. Pilch, who never married, was landlord of the Saracen's Head pub at Canterbury, and was also an umpire. Although many players ended their lives in poverty, having squandered the money they made from the game, Pilch doesn't appear to be one of them. He died in 1870, by which time cricket was the country's main summer game. Fuller Pilch was buried in the churchyard of St Gregory's, Canterbury.

Campaigning Clarksons

"He, if ever human being did it, listened exclusively to his conscience and obeyed its voice." So was Thomas Clarkson described. After a long, hard career, his moment of vindication came in 1833.

Campaigner with a conscience: The 68ft (20.6m) high 1881 Clarkson Memorial in Wisbech.

What did he do?

On the banks of the River Nene at Wisbech, by the old town bridge, you will see a giant memorial to one of the heroes of the British anti-slavery movement. Everyone has heard of William Wilberforce, but Thomas Clarkson is less well known. Yet without Clarkson there may have been no Wilberforce. In 1833 both men saw their life's work achieved.

Clarkson isn't entirely forgotten

The Fenland town's honour for its influential son was well earned. Born in 1760 at the Royal Free Grammar School in the town, where his father the Rev John Clarkson was headmaster, Thomas was intended to become an Anglican clergyman. It was while studying at Cambridge to that end that his interest in slavery began. Set an essay question on the legality of one person owning another, he researched the issue, and was horrified by what he discovered. African slavery began during the previous century to provide labour for West Indian colonies. Although Britain was not the first country to use slaves, by the second half of the 18th century much of its sugar production, for example, depended on slave labour. Slaves were shipped across the Atlantic from Africa in appalling conditions, many dying along the way.

Didn't people worry about the morality?

Like so many things, it was just accepted. Life was harsher and more precarious then, and few people had the time or luxury to bother too much about black slaves who many regarded as barely human. Many historians believe the whole British Empire was founded on the back of slavery, so it was a difficult trade to stop. But dissenting voices were beginning to be heard. The Quakers, the Society of Friends, were the first in Britain to raise moral objections; Clarkson as a young man was a friend of banker Jonathan Peckover, whose Quaker family had settled in Wisbech, and many of his confederates were also Quakers. Clarkson's conscience was pricked. It was after he had written his essay on slavery that the 25-year-old student experienced what he later called "a direct revelation from God ordering me to devote my life to abolishing the trade". His vocation to be a clergyman abandoned, Clarkson's long, hazardous journey was about to start.

Why was it hazardous?

In 1787 Clarkson was among 12 men who set up the Committee for the Abolition of the African Slave Trade. His essay had caused a stir and he now set off around the country, travelling more than 30,000 miles in seven years, in search of facts to support the campaign. In ports such as Bristol and Liverpool it was dangerous work, as slave traders and shipowners weren't keen on having the brutality of their trade exposed. On more than one occasion he was threatened, but refused to back down, and publicised what he saw. Throughout this period his workrate was prodigious, and he risked burning himself out. A physical breakdown in 1794 was the inevitable result, and he was forced to rest. Between 1787 and 1794 he had written several anti-slavery books and pamphlets; public support was beginning to grow.

What about politics?

The young William Wilberforce was MP for Hull. As such he had less to lose in opposing the slave trade. His constituents, being on the east coast, were not involved in the Atlantic slave trade. As a friend of prime minister William Pitt the Younger, he was the ideal anti-slavery spokesman, making the cause more respectable and less of a fringe issue. The campaign might have made progress earlier had the French Revolution not made the government and monarchy more nervous about any kind of liberal reform. As it was, it is to the credit of the British that they were willing to abolish a practice that was so profitable. The tide was turning slowly. In 1807 a liberal-leaning Whig government, influenced by a public campaign, passed the Abolition Act to outlaw the trade. This was not the end of the story. It took more than two decades for the institution to be abolished in the West Indies. By now the campaigners had widespread public support. At Norwich, for example, in 1825, a county meeting at the Shirehall, with the High Sheriff as president, decided to petition Parliament for the immediate abolition of slavery in British colonies. "The petition, which was presented in the House of Commons by Mr Edward Wodehouse on March 1, 1826, received 17,125 signatures and was 82 yards in length." It was not until 1833 that slavery itself was abolished; despite failing health, both Clarkson and Wilberforce lived long enough to see it. Nevertheless, it was 30 years before the USA managed the feat – and it took a civil war to force the issue.

What did Thomas Clarkson do next?

Although celebrated as a model philanthropist, his massive two-volume History of the Rise, Progress and Accomplishment of the Abolition of the African Slave Trade (1808) was criticised for downplaying the roles of other people, particularly Wilberforce. There was a cooling of the friendship between the two when some of the latter's correspondence was published. This was unfortunate, because no-one doubted Clarkson's sincerity. He continued to fight the good fight, travelling to Paris in 1818 to put in a word with the Tsar for Russia's downtrodden serfs – slaves in all but name.

Any time for a private life?

Although people driven by zeal for a cause are often hard to be around, being a little too earnest for most, Clarkson was a popular man. Six feet tall and dressed in black, a "gentle giant", he counted among his friends the Wordsworths, industrialist Josiah Wedgwood and the poet Samuel Taylor Coleridge – whose tribute to him is at the top of this story. He was fortunate to find a sympathetic wife. In 1796 he married Catherine Buck, of Bury St Edmunds. The couple lived in the Lake District before returning with their son Tom to live at Playford Hall, near Ipswich. In later life Clarkson suffered from cataracts, and almost went blind. A risky operation in 1836 restored his sight and he went on writing and reading feverishly, ignoring doctors' orders, until his death in 1846.

Anything else?

John Clarkson was the younger brother of Thomas. He also played a vital role in the anti-slavery campaign. John joined the Royal Navy aged 12, and served in the Caribbean as a lieutenant. There he would have witnessed the cruelty of the slave trade at first hand. By the age of 27 he was a committed anti-slaver. In 1791 he was sent to Nova Scotia, Canada, as the agent of the Sierra Leone Company. During the American War of Independence many black slaves sided with Britain in order to win their promised freedom. After Britain's defeat they found refuge in Canada, but a new homeland was needed for them in Africa. John Clarkson worked with the 'Black Loyalists', as they were termed, who were led by Thomas Peters. They wanted to go home to Africa, from which many of them, or their ancestors, had been abducted in the first place. In January, 1792, a fleet of 15 ships carrying nearly 1,200 people set out for Sierra Leone in west Africa. It was a terrible crossing, with bad weather and disease picking off many voyagers. Clarkson himself almost died of fever. In March, 1792, they arrived in Sierra Leone, and founded the city of Freetown.

Not quite the promised land though. . .

John Clarkson stayed as governor until December of that year. He was reckoned a fair and generous man, but life in Sierra Leone was hard for the freed slaves, who continued to be exploited. On his return to England, John lobbied on their behalf, but was dismissed by the company. A year later war broke out between Britain and revolutionary France. Clarkson, still a naval officer, was offered a ship but refused to fight. By now he believed war was wrong. Like his brother, he joined the Peace Movement. With his wife Susan he moved, first to Purfleet, Essex, and then to Woodbridge, Suffolk. They had ten children, but only four of his daughters outlived him. John Clarkson died in 1828, a few years before slavery was finally abolished. He is buried in Woodbridge.

Working class heroes?

In 1838 a national movement arrived in Norwich. To some, the Chartists were dangerous revolutionaries; to others they were working class heroes.

Who were the Chartists?

They have been described as the first mass political movement for working people in the world. Their campaign, which began in 1837, came to a head a decade later and never really ended, being seen as a template for grass roots movements worldwide. On October 28, 1838, a mass meeting in Norwich Market Place saw the 'People's Charter' launched in Norfolk. Founding members Joseph Stephens and Julian Harney outlined the movement's demands. These were condensed into 'six points': universal suffrage for all men over 21; equal-sized electoral constituencies; secret ballots; no property qualification for MPs; pay for MPs; and annual parliaments. Founded by London artisans the previous year, and taken up by an Irish journalist and activist named Fergus O'Connor, Chartism was a disparate movement uniting many labouring people, mainly from industrial areas, under its banner. It was particularly strong in the industrial north and midlands, where a growing labouring population gave it numbers and strength. In the end, disunity would be its downfall – but its ideals lived on.

What happened in Norwich?

The city, a hotbed of radicalism for generations, was in economic recession during the 1830s. Its traditional weaving trade had been undercut by war from the 1790s onwards and increasing competition from northern industrial regions. Nevertheless, it proved fertile ground for Chartists. Many working people had supported the Whig Reform Act of 1832, which had benefited the middle classes, but subsequently felt betrayed by their exclusion from power. However, most Chartists saw reform of Parliament as the way to improve the conditions of the working classes. It was, as Joseph Stephens told his audience, "a knife and fork, bread and cheese question". Although the authorities were nervous of mass meetings, Norwich's mayor gave permission for St Andrew's Hall to be used for a subsequent meeting the day following the Market Place event.

Everyone on the same side then?

Chartists were split between those who believed in 'moral force' and 'physical force'. In 1839, after a mass petition to Parliament was rejected out of hand by MPs, violence of the physical sort broke out in Newport, Wales. Chartists tried to seize public buildings in a bid to spark a national uprising. In Norwich, John Dover, "the keeper of a beer shop in St Paul's", became the Chartist spokesman. His favoured tactic, according to hostile contemporary accounts, was to disrupt public meetings. For example, early in 1839 Chartists disrupted a city council Corn Law repeal meeting, much to Mayor Marshall's chagrin. By March of that year, fears were spreading that the Chartists were arming themselves to take power. "It is said that about 60 will leave Norwich armed with pikes and other weapons, some of them with pistols, for the north of England." Although these reports were quickly dismissed as scaremongering, in August Chartists arranged meetings on Mousehold Heath. Police swore in special constables and the West Norfolk militia were put on standby. In the event the closest Norwich came to a revolution was when some Chartists gatecrashed a service at St Stephen's Church – and hissed the preacher. Others asked the vicar of St Simon and Jude, the Rev John Owen, to read a text to them, "and the greatest order prevailed" among a large congregation. "Hundreds were unable to gain admission in consequence of the crowd." That said, the Bishop of Norwich was "assailed by the mob". John Dover was arrested on a charge of ordering a smith to make weapons.

A man of the people?

To the rattled authorities he became "Dover, the notorious Chartist". He gave great offence at the Guildhall. The mayor had called a meeting to send a message of congratulation to the young Queen Victoria on avoiding an attempted assassination. "Dover and a party of Norwich Chartists occupied a gallery and created much disturbance," wrote a reporter. Similarly, Dover upset an anti-slavery meeting at St Andrew's Hall by claiming British workers were treated no better than slaves. On another occasion a meeting to protest at the new Poor Law was hijacked by Dover's Chartists; although they were trying to make some serious points, it all ended in mob violence when the mayor and "other gentlemen were besieged in the Norfolk Hotel". Dover's career went horribly wrong in June, 1841. At another Guildhall meeting to determine who would stand as Norwich MP, he was accused by his fellow Chartists of 'selling out' by accepting a £50 bribe to withdraw a Chartist candidate. Things got out of hand. A mob waylaid him outside the Guildhall, in Dove Lane, while the police on duty were "assailed by a volley of brickbats and other missiles", and the militia arrived in force. The following day Dover was dragged from his home in Colegate, "brutally belaboured" and was only saved from being thrown into the river by the pleadings of one of his children. Eventually, he was rescued by the mayor and a party of soldiers, who bundled him into a coach and whisked him to the relative safety of the city jail. The city was in uproar for two days until "public tranquility was somewhat restored by a procession in which Philip Augustus, the musical pieman and Jerry, the lucifer match seller, in a military costume, with an immense plume of feathers in his cap were 'chaired'." Things got even worse for Dover four years later. Convicted of receiving stolen silk goods, he was transported to Australia for 14 years.

There's a moral there somewhere. . .

Being a Chartist was perilous. O'Connor and the two earlier Norwich speakers, Stephens and Harney, all did jail time in the 1840s. They remained popular; in July, 1847, O'Connor drew a large attendance at a public meeting at St Andrew's Hall. The national movement came to a head in 1848. A 'monster meeting' was held in London. The government feared revolution; the aged Duke of Wellington was called out of retirement, troops mobilised and thousands of special constables sworn in, threatening the Chartists with a crackdown if they crossed the River Thames. O'Connor and some colleagues eventually presented a petition with 1.9 million signatures to Parliament. MPs rejected it, claiming many were forgeries. A Chartist Convention met – supposedly an alternative Parliament. Samuel Francis was the Ipswich delegate; William Dixon represented Norwich. More 'moral' than 'physical' force Chartists, the Convention quickly dissolved into chaos and mutual acrimony. Although accused by hardliners of losing his nerve, O'Connor became MP for Nottingham. In 1849, now thoroughly respectable, he joined other MPs to address a reform meeting at Norwich's St Andrew's Hall. Sadly, he was later certified a lunatic and died six years later. In a way the Chartists had the last laugh. By 1918 all but one of their demands – that for annual Parliaments – had become law.

19th century **1840**

Utopia in Manea

Farmland in the middle of the Fens seems like an unlikely place to build a perfect society – but in the middle of the 19th century a group of idealists believed they could do it.

Society was far from perfect at the time?

Life for the poor was hard – and getting harder. Landless farm labourers struggled to make a living, particularly when the introduction of new machinery, along with periodic economic slumps, put them out of work. Many gravitated to the growing cities, where work could be found in the new factories but conditions were as insanitary and difficult as those in the country. In the Fens discontent was growing. It culminated in the Littleport riots of 1816, while the introduction of new workhouses brought about by the 1834 Poor Law Amendment was much hated. The poor, lacking education, also lacked a voice. But they were not entirely abandoned. Middle class idealists were horrified by what they saw. Among them was industrialist Robert Owen. "Man's character is formed by his environment," he wrote. Starting with creating a model village at New Lanark in Scotland, he went on to found further utopian ventures to put his principles into action. Owen aroused strong reactions; to some a foolish and dangerous revolutionary, to others a visionary genius. He spread his co-operative ideas to the eastern counties. In July, 1838, he gave a series of lectures at St Andrew's Hall, Norwich, outlining "his visionary projects for a new organisation and classification of society".

And in Wisbech?

The town of Wisbech had a history of dissent and free-thinking. Owen had at least one devoted follower in the town. James Hill, son of a wealthy Peterborough farmer, was by profession a corn merchant. But by conviction he was a reformer, and a fearless enemy of what he considered injustice and inequality. Unafraid of making enemies, he founded a liberal newspaper, The Star in the East, dedicated to "help forward the cause of humanity", which brought him into conflict with the authorities. Along with his second wife

Caroline Southwood, he founded a progressive school for poor children "free from vice, error and superstition". To landowners and employers he added the Church of England, which was alarmed at the thought of revolutionary doctrines spreading to the children of farm labourers, to his long list of critics. He also founded his own bank.

Any local support?

James and Caroline were convinced Owenites, and were not alone in their views. When the man himself visited Wisbech in 1838, up to 500 people gathered to hear him speak. Among others enthused by Owen's vision was William Hodson. An Upwell farmer and lay Methodist preacher, he bought 200 acres of land near the village of Manea, 10 miles from Wisbech. The Central Board of Owenites decided his project to found a communistic, self-sufficient farming community there was unfeasible, but that did not deter him. With the backing – both moral and probably financial – of James Hill, Hodson went ahead with the scheme. In July, 1839, a hundred or more colonists marched to Manea to found their co-operative community.

Who were they?

Many were idealists, early socialists with an optimistic view of human nature. Others may have seen the colony simply as a place for a better life. Their principles were impeccable; adopting the motto "each for all", the colonists made themselves modern cottages built of brick, with central heating. They also built a pavilion and windmill. A schoolroom staffed by teachers was provided for their children. In the fields, where workers would toil for just four hours each day, music would be provided. The colony was constructed on the west side of the Old Bedford River, so had access to water transport, and the colonists could also use a pleasure craft provided for the purpose. Money was abolished. Vouchers could be spent at the community shop. A periodical, The Working Bee, was produced by the colonists, who wore a 'uniform' of Lincoln green.

Couldn't fail. Could it?

Unfortunately for those who believe human nature is perfectible, the community was riven by dissent. Perhaps when dissenters, non-conformists and free-thinkers are thrown together, it is inevitable. One imagines there were a few large egos bruising one another. The idealists, many of whom were town people unused to working the land, clashed with the easy-lifers, the site suffered flooding due to drainage problems and markets for goods were hard to find. Local people, perhaps understandably, were suspicious of the incomers. They had the reputation of dangerous radicals, and didn't really help their cause by flying a French tricolor above the Union Flag as a symbol of liberty. Hodson got into financial difficulties, probably when James Hill's bank folded, and withdrew support. Within a few years the colony was finished. For James Hill things were even worse. After his bank and newspaper failed, along with other co-operative ventures, he suffered a nervous breakdown from which he never truly recovered, and had to leave Wisbech. His family carved out a new life in London, and his daughter Octavia inherited her parents' reforming zeal. Beginning with managing what we would now call 'social housing' in the capital she became one of the founders of the National Trust later in the century – as we will see in a later chapter. Her childhood home in Wisbech has been turned into a museum, where you can see a scale model of what the colony may have looked like. The museum also houses fascinating period detail.

What happened to the colony?

Utopian schemes have never really thrived in Britain. During and just after the English Civil Wars groups of idealists made attempts to create more equal societies. The Levellers, many of whom were New Model Army soldiers, were crushed in the 1640s. Their civilian counterparts the Diggers, who believed that goods should be held in common, made little headway. So it was with the Manea colony, which soon folded. Local people took over the disused land. But an echo of the 1840s came following the First World War. Cambridgeshire County Council bought what became known as Colony Farm and provided smallholdings for returning soldiers to work the land and become self-sufficient. A very different model village was founded at Thorney, near Peterborough, a few years later. This time its patron was an aristocrat, the Duke of Bedford, who settled descendants of French Huguenot refugees there. Lacking the Owenites' idealism, but with a generous backer, this venture succeeded. Read into that what you will. . .

Octavia Hill Birthplace Museum, 1 South Brink Place, Wisbech.
The Manea colony site is at OS grid reference TL515920.

The railways come east

In the mid-19th century railways changed eastern England. Before their arrival communities existed in relative isolation; afterwards things were never the same again.

And not universally popular?

As with all radical change, there were winners and losers – and those who lost out could hardly have been expected to welcome the innovation. So it was in the Norfolk of the 1840s. The county, and East Anglia in general, had been falling behind fast industrialising parts of the country, and its economy, wealth and influence had declined. The railway industry had its birth in the north, and the subsequent creation of successful railways linking the midlands to London demonstrated the speed and cost-cutting benefits of rail. East Anglia had to catch up quickly.

What were the benefits locally?

In Great Yarmouth in particular they were chomping at the bit. They had all this lovely fresh fish spilling on to the dockside, and all those hungry customers in London just waiting for it to arrive. But to get the product to the capital meant a slow journey by river wherry to Norwich and beyond. Other businesses, including those selling meat to Smithfield who had to drive animals to market by road, and even Norwich's ailing cloth trade, could see the attractions of speedy rail connections. From the mid-1830s various railway schemes were put forward, but little was done.

Why the delay?

Building a railway cost a lot of money; an initial estimate of £200,000 to build the 20 or so miles of the Norwich-Yarmouth railway proved way too low. Before the actual building there was the cost of buying land and compensating owners, getting an Act of Parliament to legitimise the venture – then there were subsequent running costs. Before getting the say-so, railway promoters had to prove it could be built, so engineers and surveyors like George Parker Bidder had to go over every mile of land and demonstrate to a sceptical audience how the thing would be done. During the 1830s a trade slump, particularly in agriculture, discouraged investors. In the early 1840s though a number of schemes reached fruition; from the south the Eastern Union worked to link London to East Anglia via Ipswich. In the east the Norwich and Yarmouth Railway finally became reality. Stagecoach operators and wherry owners stood to be put out of business by railways, but there was little they could do. Landowners on the proposed route could prove a real obstacle to development, and a number held out for more compensation, resulting in lengthy court cases. Some people had more idealistic reasons for disliking railways. Romantic novel writer George Borrow, author of Romany Rye, was not alone in fearing what modern communications would do to his beloved rural Norfolk, and he denounced the railways.

They didn't stop the railways being built though!

Some genuine heavyweights entered the frame, bringing cash, talent and knowhow. George Stephenson's accomplished engineer son Robert surveyed the Norwich-Yarmouth route, while financier George Hudson, the 'Railway King', was involved from the London end. Contractor Samuel Morton Peto really got things moving, first in Norfolk and then Suffolk, where he settled at Somerleyton in 1845. This daring entrepreneur, initially trained as a civil engineer, represented the Stephensons in their attempt to extend the rail network from north to south. After frantic borrowing and some bold promises, Peto persuaded his East Anglian backers. George Bidder answered the technical questions, and swayed the public meetings. With the legal side settled and cash in place, the first sod was cut at Postwick Hall Farm, near Thorpe, in March, 1843. By May a new canal was cut at Thorpe St Andrew, and work was under way at the difficult site of Reedham by the river.

Any other problems?

It was not long before complaints began about 'navvies' (navigators) and their heavy drinking. Peto acted quickly. A religious non-Conformist, he was a genuinely philanthropic employer who offered contracts and a savings bank for his workers, but he also demanded – and got – discipline from his men. The marshland west of Yarmouth proved a more intractable problem, and it took months for the navigators to dig their way out of the Yare valley.

Nevertheless, the railway opened on time on May 1, 1844. The new Norwich station at Thorpe, then outside the city's built-up area, was the scene of formal celebrations. This was not today's grand modern station – that was built in the 1880s – but a more rudimentary affair. A carriage containing civicl dignitaries and a brass band set out for a day at the seaside. 'Railway Mania' took off everywhere. Norwich was linked to Lowestoft, then to London via Brandon, and a new station built at Queens Road; this Norwich Victoria was the initial terminal for London trains. It later acted as a goods station before demolition in the 1980s. A modern Sainsbury's store marks the site. Although promoters had not stressed it, and perhaps did not originally see it coming, the most noticeable benefit was the beginning of mass tourism. In summer, 1846 a 52-carriage train carried an estimated 2,000 passengers from London to Great Yarmouth, via Norwich, paying 7s 6d for a week's return. That same year trains took some 3,000 children from chapel schools in Norwich and Norfolk to Yarmouth.

Everyone happy then?

Passengers and business users were soon complaining about lateness, breakdowns, mismanagement and accidents caused by excessive speed. No change there then. On Christmas Eve, 1845, a train travelling at 55mph derailed between Thetford and Attleborough, killing the driver, Pickering, and the stoker, Richard Eager; the worst of many shunts. Conditions on the trains were not always inviting; third class accommodation initially consisted of backless benches open to the elements. Despite these problems, and financial crises in which individual companies folded, the railways were here to stay, and the groundwork of a national network was laid. In 1862 East Anglian lines were amalgamated into the Great Eastern Railway.

Entrepreneur: A bust of Samuel Morton Peto stands at Norwich Railway Station.

The first weatherman

A few years ago listeners to BBC Radio 4's shipping forecast learnt a new name. Fitzroy replaced Finisterre as one of the areas on the weather map. Who was Robert Fitzroy? Here is the tale of a tragic figure, shipmate and friend of Charles Darwin, colonial governor and the father of modern weather forecasting, which began in 1860.

Darwin's friend? An evolutionist then. . .

Robert Fitzroy was a Royal Navy captain, a brilliant sailor and navigator – but not an evolutionist. Certainly not. Unlike Charles Darwin, Fitzroy never questioned his devout religious faith. He was born at Ampton Hall, near Bury St Edmunds, in 1805, part of the distinguished aristocratic Grafton family. Robert was a great-grandson of King Charles II via an illegitimate line: his uncle Viscount Castlereagh was Foreign Secretary in the early 1800s. (He was the one the poet Lord Byron didn't like; *"I met murder on the way/He had a mask like Castlereagh"*). This distinguished ancestry gave Robert Fitzroy a head-start in life, but he also had talent. Like Horatio Nelson and John Clarkson, he entered the naval world aged 12 when he attended the Royal Naval College, Portsmouth. He joined the Navy the following year. At 19 he passed his examination with 'full numbers' – a feat never accomplished before – and was promoted to lieutenant, marked for great things. Four years later he was serving in South American waters when a golden opportunity arose.

Involving a certain Mr Darwin?

Fitzroy was appointed captain of HMS Beagle following the suicide of the previous skipper. The mission was to conduct a survey of Tierra del Fuego on the tip of South America. An incident in 1830 illustrates Fitzroy's character. He brought back four of the indigenous people to England. There, one of them died of smallpox, and Fitzroy was determined to return the survivors to their homes, and succeeded in so doing. His captaincy of the Beagle confirmed in 1831, Fitzroy prepared to sail south again. This time he took with him a naturalist and companion. After the first candidate dropped out, 22-year-old

Charles Darwin stepped in. He and Fitzroy were to sail together for the next five years. Travelling around the tip of South America they visited the Galapagos Islands, Tahiti, New Zealand, Australia and southern Africa before returning to England via the Atlantic and a detour to Brazil.

How did they get on?

Both were young men and, despite various theological arguments during their long voyage, they became friends. Darwin described Fitzroy as a man of considerable charm and liberal views. The charm, however, could be clouded by a violent temper and some very dark depressions. These character traits would return in later life with terrible consequences. Fitzroy's own account of the Pacific voyage, which lasted until 1836, reflected some of the themes which would later cause a rift between the two. He was a firm believer in the version of the Creation by God described in the Bible; Darwin's discoveries in the Pacific were to become the basis of his theory of evolution by natural selection, which undermined that faith in the Almighty. For now Fitzroy's career, boosted by his excellent captaincy of the Beagle in difficult and barely charted waters, thrived. Newly married, on his return to England he was elected Tory MP for Durham. But he soon set sail again.

Back to the Pacific?

He was appointed Governor of New Zealand in 1843. It proved a poisoned chalice. According to one reporter, "a more thorny path he could hardly have taken". Settlers in the new colony were pushing for more land, the native Maoris were resisting. Fitzroy tried to hold the line between them, and uphold a treaty protecting Maori lands. It proved impossible, and war soon broke out. Commercial interests in England were critical of Fitzroy's 'soft' line, and he was replaced in 1848. His political career was at an end, but he was still a serving naval officer. Far from disgraced in the eyes of the Navy, he became superintendent of the Royal Naval Dockyards at Woolwich, then commander of the frigate HMS Argonaut. His retirement from active service on health grounds in 1851 did not mark the end of his career. The newly promoted Vice-Admiral Fitzroy took on a new department, one that affected all mariners. The weather.

He became the first weatherman?

Fitzroy's new job was as Meteorological Statist to the Board of Trade with a staff of three, the forerunner of the modern Meteorological Office. Fitzroy took the job on, and reinvented it. Ship captains provided him with information to compile weather data, and Fitzroy designed and distributed a barometer to every port to be consulted by crews before they set sail. Stone housings for such barometers are still visible at many ports. By the end of the 1850s Fitzroy had developed charts to predict storms at sea, and land stations were established using the newly invented telegraph to feed him regular updates. He became famous. Satirical magazine Punch dubbed him "The First Admiral of the Blew". The first daily weather 'forecasts' – a word he invented – were published in The Times in 1860, and his Weather Book first published soon afterwards. Many fishermen in particular felt the gale warnings posted in harbours that prevented them sailing actually saved their lives, so to them Fitzroy was a hero. But his reputation was a double-edged sword. The technology was in its infancy; when things went wrong he was widely blamed. A modern TV weather would understand!

What about Darwin?

Charles Darwin agonised for years over his findings and their contradiction of the Bible. A frequent visitor to his home in Kent was his friend Fitzroy, and we can imagine the discussions that went on. But when Darwin finally published Origin of Species, Fitzroy felt betrayed. In June, 1860, he was invited to Oxford University to speak on the weather. By chance it was the occasion of a famous evolution debate between Thomas Huxley and the Bishop of Oxford, 'Soapy Sam' Wilberforce. Outraged, Fitzroy interrupted. Brandishing the Bible in both hands, the tall, grey-haired admiral declared: "Here is the truth – in here!" Shouted down by students, he was led dejected from the building. Burdened by illness and deafness, hurt by criticism of his weather forecasts, worried by financial pressures, but mostly weighed down by a sense of failure over Darwin, Fitzroy became depressed. On April 30, 1865 he rose early without waking his wife, kissed his daughter, then cut his throat with a razor in exact duplication of his uncle Castlereagh's suicide in 1822.

And the shipping forecast?

In 2002 Fitzroy became the new name for the area formerly known as Finisterre, between Trafalgar, Biscay and Sole. The name was changed to avoid confusion with a Spanish area of the same name. A fitting tribute to a principled man who did his best to save lives at sea.

Gypsy king of the ring

A travelling man?

In 1870 boxer James 'Jem' Mace was acclaimed champion of the world following his victory in a fight in the USA. Mace was born in Norfolk, lived in America and Australia and is buried in Liverpool – he got around. He was the last of the great bare-knuckle boxers, and merits a mention along with the likes of Muhammed Ali in the international Boxing Hall of Fame. He was still giving displays into his seventies before dying a pauper's death.

Bare-knuckle? He must have been a tough man

But a real sportsman, and something of a gentleman if all accounts are to be believed, though he rubbed shoulders with all sorts in his colourful and eventful life. He was born at Beeston, Norfolk, in April, 1831, the son of a blacksmith said to be of gypsy descent, though Mace later denied he had Romany roots. His career began in the 1850s when he was spotted boxing at a Norwich fair. Before long he was touring with Nat Langham's professional troupe. They travelled around country fairs giving demonstrations in roped-off areas. These were rough and ready affairs; local likely lads would turn up hoping to get the better of the pros. The flamboyant Jem was too good for them; he only admitted to two defeats in his career. He also played the violin at country dances. Before long his reputation was growing, and he was fighting for championships.

Boxing was a free-for-all in those days

It certainly had a raffish reputation, but it was a sport that appealed to all classes of society. Boxing gained the backing of 'The Fancy', an unlikely fraternity of well-heeled aristocrats with sporting instincts, including the likes of the poet Lord Byron, and gnarled fighters from the wrong side of the tracks. In the previous generation the Prince of Wales had been an admirer of the pioneering fighter Daniel Mendoza. Huge crowds estimated at more than 20,000 were attracted to top matches – quite something considering there were no mass communications then. Although bare-knuckle fights with no limits on the number of rounds could be bloody, a code of rules and sportsmanship applied. Mace was considered a 'scientific' boxer, using fast footwork and defensive tactics to outwit opponents. Unusually for the times, he made pre-match notes about opponents. Because of this his modern admirers dub him "the father of modern boxing". Mace toughened his fists by 'pickling' them in a solution of whisky, gunpowder and hedgehog fat to prevent bruising and swelling. Boxers such as Bob Thorpe, Posh Price, Bob Travers and Bob Brettle all felt the force of those fists, falling to him until, in 1861, he won the English Championship from Sam Hurst in a bout held at Medway Island, Kent. The following year he defended his title, but lost to Tom King in 43 rounds. It had been such a close fight that he demanded a rematch. Eventually he was to win both the Middleweight and Heavyweight titles, before retiring in 1870.

And that was that?

Hardly. Ever the showman, Jem took off for the USA with his own travelling show. Although he did not intend to enter the ring himself, when Tom Allen, the American champion, hove into view he could not resist a match that would make the victor 'Champion of the World'. Actually, both men had been born in England, but that was no rarity at the time as many British and Irish boxers crossed the Atlantic, and dominated the sport. So, in the spring of 1870, on the banks of the Mississippi near New Orleans, the boy from Beeston took on the world – and won. In front of a massive crowd of excited onlookers a hard-fought battle ended in the 10th round when Allen's arm was dislocated. In a gesture of mutual respect, 40-year-old Mace walked to his corner, clapped the younger Allen on the back, and declared: "Tom, you are a game man and I wish you well." This was one of the last bare-knuckle fights in history. The Marquis of Queensberry's 1867 code was rapidly adopted, and that included wearing gloves. Bare-knuckle fights were outlawed, so protagonists ran the risk of arrest.

So Jem settled down into retirement?

Not the retiring sort. Promoting the new Queensberry Rules, he gave exhibition matches with the great American John L Sullivan on a tour of the States in 1884, and even had a last tilt at the British title when he lost to Charlie Mitchell. He was aged 58 by then. In between he lived in Australia in the early 1880s, influencing a whole generation of fighters. In New Zealand he trained Bob FitzSimmons. He was a young fighter, originally from Cornwall, whose family had emigrated to New Zealand. FitzSimmons went on to become boxing's first three-division world champion. For a while he trained at Mace's boxing school.

Hopefully, Jem was looking after his money

He was not. By one account, he "spent it all on women and horses". So, at least, he didn't waste it. While in the USA he was said to have run a saloon in New York city; while in Australia he had a hotel in Melbourne. The money rolled in, and it rolled out. Mace is said to have married three times – twice bigamously – and fathered a total of 14 children. That's the legend, at all events. In old age, he fell on hard times. He had to sell his championship belts, and relied on the charity of his friends. Mace was still physically fit – a photograph taken of him in his seventies shows a cheerful looking face unscarred by his many fights. At least he earned money from promotional bouts; in 1908 this popular character returned to his home county to referee a tournament at the Theatre Royal, Norwich. But within two years he was dead of pneumonia. He died at Jarrow in the north-east, and his body was taken to Liverpool where he had owned a fairground known as the Strawberry Gardens, in the Anfield area of the city. It was there on Merseyside he was buried, in an unmarked grave, on December 10, 1910.

A sad end

But he was not forgotten. There is a stone cross dedicated to him in the graveyard at Beeston and a lifesized statue of him and Allen at LaSalles Landing, 12 miles from New Orleans. In 2002 a group of former boxers got together to buy a headstone for his Liverpool grave. As the Liverpool Daily Post reported, a silver inscription reads: "He stood unconquered, champion of the field. Time counts him out. But memory will remain. We ne'er will look upon his like again."

Anything else?

Mace was licencee of the White Swan pub, in Swan Lane, Norwich, in the late 1850s. In 1858 he was charged with threatening language used to Mrs Mary Ann Stowers in a dispute over money owed to her husband. Mace was bound over by city magistrates to keep the peace. The pub disappeared well over a century ago, and the site is currently a restaurant.

19th century **1895**

Trust in Octavia

She was a woman who succeeded in a man's world. A pioneer whose ideas have influenced how people live and see the world around them – and you can see where it all began for her in Wisbech. In 1895 she was one of the founders of the National Trust, which continues to thrive today.

Who was Octavia Hill and what did she do?

Born on the banks of the River Nene in 1838, Octavia Hill was a Victorian social worker. Trying to help the urban poor lead a better and healthier life, she became a co-founder of the National Trust, a campaigner for open spaces as well as creating a new profession of housing management. Her birthplace on the South Brink of the Nene is a substantial, but by no means grand, building. Although Octavia only lived there until she was two years old, her roots were in the fenland town. The house has been converted into a museum telling the story of her life, her family and the influences upon her.

A wealthy family?

Octavia's parents were James and Caroline Hill. They were radical liberals with opinions that put them at odds with a conservative establishment. James, a banker in competition with the better known Peckovers, whose mansion stood directly opposite on the North Brink, was an idealist. He was influenced by the great philanthropist Robert Owen, whose utopian model communities saw property held in common and social rank abolished. James, who moved from banking to the corn business, founded the area's first newspaper, The Star in the East, which attacked what he saw as corruption. The couple also founded a school where the Angles Theatre stands. It was dedicated to teaching poor children who were otherwise unschooled; both ventures made them enemies. James Hill went bankrupt and suffered a breakdown from which he never recovered. Excerpts from his newspaper dedicated to telling "The Truth, the whole Truth and nothing but the Truth" and other cuttings tell the story. An important friend of the Hill family was the utilitarian philosopher Jeremy Bentham. On his death, Bentham's body was left to

Octavia Hill's grandfather, Dr Thomas Southwood Smith. On Bentham's instructions he dissected it, wired up the skeleton and put it in Bentham's clothes as a memorial. The original can be seen in University College, London (where he was recorded for years following his death as 'present but not voting').

What did the family do next?

They left Wisbech in 1840 to live with grandfather Smith. Living in rural Finchley, Octavia and her sisters enjoyed an idyllic childhood. But these were serious people, not given to a frivolous lifestyle. Moving to London in her early teens the slums where the poor lived had a great impact on Octavia. Aged 25, she entered the orbit of John Ruskin, for whom she had made copies of original artwork. This artist turned social campaigner was also appalled at the living conditions of the London poor. When he bought a notorious slum ironically called Paradise Place – otherwise known as 'Little Hell' – he appointed Octavia to run it. In the museum, a one-room apartment has been recreated. Using models of a typical family – based on the 1861 census, contemporary illustrations and journalist Henry Mayhew's accounts – the display shows seven people living in damp, cramped conditions. Hill encouraged the creation of small open spaces to bring "the healthy gift of air and joy of plants and flowers". A determined character, she was hard but fair. She was not interested in dishing out charity, but fostering a Victorian spirit of self-reliance and self-help among the poor. Her aim was to make "lives noble, homes happy, and family life good". She felt personal, friendly and supportive management could improve slum areas and create communities, a view borne out by the results; the properties also made a profit. She influenced a generation of housing workers.

What about the National Trust?

Octavia Hill was one of the founders of the National Trust in 1895 "for the preservation of natural beauty and buildings of historical interest". The National Trust today has two million members and half a million acres of land. She was the first to use the phrase 'green belt' to describe the practice of creating open space around cities. The Octavia Hill Society set up the volunteer-run museum, at 1 South Brink Place, in 1995.

20th century **1906**

'Our George'

Fight the good fight, with all thy might

Stirring words
Taken from Sir George Edwards's favourite hymn, they illustrate his life. From illiterate ploughboy he became a knight of the realm, and made his life's work the improvement of the lot of his fellow farmworkers. A union leader and devout Methodist lay preacher, he was remembered in Norfolk as 'our George'. In 1906 he helped form the first successful agricultural workers' trade union in East Anglia. But his faith was sorely tested in a hard life in which his was a voice of moderation and forgiveness in turbulent times.

Life on the land was always hard
George was born in 1850 at Marsham, near Aylsham, in conditions of real poverty. Father Robert was a farmworker who found employment hard to obtain during the 'Hungry Forties'. Mother Mary often went without so her children could eat. Aged six, young George was sent to work crow scaring. The hours were long for a lad so young – when the farmer caught him sleeping he beat him. George's mother found out and slapped the farmer's face. Local magistrates were unsympathetic; she was fined. A kind friend paid the fine or she would have been jailed. When George's father was caught stealing turnips from his employer to feed his family he was jailed. His wife and children had to seek relief in the workhouse.

A hard upbringing
George had no childhood education, combining farm work with brickmaking. Wages were something like threepence a day, and in the days before mechanisation all was done by hand. He supplemented his income with poaching. Instead of turning to drink or despair as many did, aged 19 he underwent a conversion to Primitive Methodism. He also met Charlotte Corke while working at Alby. They were soon married, and she taught George to read and write; he gave up tobacco to buy books. It is often said the British

labour movement owed more to Methodism than to Marx, with its message of self-help and belief in people's essential goodness. Edwards was determined to help improve the material and spiritual state of his class. In 1872, when farmworkers rose up, he became an activist.

An uprising?

It was notoriously hard for farmworkers to organise. Scattered throughout the country, lacking education, which made communications difficult, often dependant on employers for housing, they also faced legal hostility. But in 1872 midlander Joseph Arch formed an agricultural workers' union. George was keen to join his national organisation, but the Norfolk workers showed characteristic 'do different' independence by going it alone. It proved a tactical mistake. In the wave of strikes and lockouts which followed in a bid to increase wages union disunity spelt eventual defeat. Disheartened, many workers drifted away and unions folded. By the early 1890s, weakened by internal division and agricultural depression, Arch's union was on its last legs. Disillusioned, he told Edwards to "never trust our class again".

But Edwards kept the faith

He walked and later cycled to hundreds of meetings from his Fakenham home, enrolling members. But his union activities got him into trouble with his employers, more than once resulting in his dismissal. Employers resorted to "locking out" strikers and employing non-union – so-called "blackleg" – labour. Violence was in the air. Although he always called for calm, and had no personal bitterness towards opponents, Edwards was threatened frequently. During the early 1900s, briefly disillusioned with the union, he became involved in local politics, at parish and district council level, and also spoke on behalf of the Liberals on the then controversial issue of Free Trade. He found work with the sympathetic Mr Ketton, a leading Liberal and owner of Felbrigg Hall, near Cromer.

But Edwards was a union man at heart

In July, 1906 he was approached by local men keen to relaunch the union. Encouraged by his wife, he agreed to help. At the Angel Hotel, North Walsham, the Eastern Counties Agricultural Labourers' and Smallholders' Union was born. Edwards warned of hard times ahead, as the employers' attitude had not softened. He was not wrong; strikes in 1910 at Trunch and St

Faiths were bitter, and the movement was hampered by acrimonious internal divisions. A severe depression hit British farming in the 1920s, worsening relations between employers and workers. Another drawn-out strike over wages in 1923 proved hard. As the strike became bitter, 100 pickets went on trial at Walsingham. Edwards was himself a magistrate, and insisted on attending court to see justice done. His calming presence helped prevent a riot as hundreds of sympathisers gathered outside. He also supported Tom and Annie Higdon, the non-conformist Burston schoolteachers whose pupils began their celebrated strike in 1914. By now his health was an issue. The death of his wife in 1912 affected him badly, as she had always supported him, and his active life increasingly caught up with him. By the end of the First World War, though, Edwards was a widely respected local figure.

And a knighthood?

He had spoken before a Royal Commission as early as 1893, headed by the future King Edward VII, in which he had outlined the plight of the farmworkers. His subsequent work led to him becoming an OBE in 1919. Now a Labour Party member, Edwards stood for the South Norfolk constituency at a by-election in 1920, and was elected. In his maiden speech in Parliament, delivered in his distinctive Norfolk dialect, he spoke about the impact of tied cottages. Although defeated at the subsequent election, he was re-elected in 1923 with an 861-strong majority, and helped form the first Labour Government. He was again defeated the following year, and did not stand for Parliament again. He was knighted in 1930 for services to agricultural workers. Ever a modest man, he insisted his fellow Fakenham town councillors still called him 'George' (though he insisted on his title being used by one landowner who he felt had once treated him with disrespect). A Labour stalwart, he considered the forming of Ramsay MacDonald's National Government during the economic recession of 1931 a betrayal.

He didn't forget his Norfolk roots

In 1933, he finally achieved victory in a long-desired project of getting playing fields built at Fakenham. It was a sweet moment. George Edwards died, aged 83, in December that year. His funeral at Buckenham Memorial Methodist Church in Fakenham drew hundreds of mourners from all walks of life. For many years a service of remembrance was held each May Day at his graveside; in 1949 Labour Prime Minister Clement Attlee attended.

Operation Pied Piper

In September, 1939, railway stations across Britain were full of evacuated children. In scenes never witnessed before or since, they were being sent away from home for safety. Many came to rural East Anglia. Their lives would never be the same again.

War clouds gathering. . .

"The bomber will always get through". So declared Prime Minister Stanley Baldwin in 1932. There could be no better illustration of the fears that gripped Britain during the 1930s of what modern war would be like – and that vulnerable people in cities and towns were at risk. By 1938 war looked likely, and the government drew up plans to evacuate schoolchildren and mothers with children under five years old from cities like London, Birmingham, Manchester and Liverpool. The country was divided into zones – 'evacuation', 'neutral' and 'reception' – by officials who decided to act on the assumption that war would begin with aerial attacks on cities. They were profoundly affected by the bombing of Spanish cities such as Guernica in that country's civil war. In February, 1939, as the international situation deteriorated, the government initiated evacuation plans. In July leaflets were sent to parents urging them to register children in advance. When Hitler's Germany invaded Poland on September 1, 1939, Operation Pied Piper was put into action. Two days later war was declared.

What happened in Norfolk?

Up to 50,000 people were earmarked to go to safe areas of the county. Ports such as Great Yarmouth and Lowestoft were considered at risk from bombing – rightly, as it turned put. On September 1 the Eastern Daily Press of Norwich, along with newspapers across the country, printed evacuation details. Detraining centres were designated at Norwich, where up to 21,000 were destined to arrive at Thorpe Station, King's Lynn, Thetford, Diss, Downham Market, New Hunstanton and Swaffham. Food and blankets were stockpiled in anticipation. General store Garlands, of London Street, Norwich, ran adverts in the EDP, declaring: "Our advice is to buy NOW for the colder months. Even if blankets are obtainable later, prices will certainly be higher." Throughout that first weekend of September they came. To the raw emotions of parting with families was added the uncertainty of not knowing where children were being sent. Many were given stamped addressed letters to send to their parents telling them where they had been settled. They were also issued with gas masks; many people feared the war would start with chemical attacks. At Downham, for example, 1,100 arrived, mainly secondary schoolchildren, followed by 300 mothers and small children. They were dispersed by road to homes where they would be billeted. Among the children were Jewish refugees from Europe. To the culture shock of city meeting country was added a language problem. A further 1,000 children came from Essex to Dereham. Inevitably there was some muddle as so many people were on the move. Whole schools arrived along with their teachers. For example, Hackney Downs School were sent to Upwell and Outwell, having arrived at King's Lynn.

A smooth operation?

Lady Bury, county organiser of the Women's Voluntary Service, was quoted in the EDP: "Success. . . depends on people letting their humanitarian ideals overcome their natural desire for an easy-going life". By and large she was not to be disappointed. At the village of Gooderstone, near Swaffham, three small children were among those evacuated out of Hackney in the East End of London, along with their entire school. They were my mother, then aged five, and her elder sister and brother. The children were taken to the village hall, where local women arrived to choose children to take home. A dairy farmer's wife was at first willing only to take the two girls, but my then nine-year-old uncle, aware of his mother's parting words not to be split up from his sisters, persuaded her to take all three. Kindly, she did, and somehow the family coped, making up a bed for my uncle in the bath that first night. A rather more famous evacuee from London was Maurice Micklewhite. Aged seven, he was a pupil at North Runcton School, near King's Lynn, where he stayed with his family until the end of the war. Maurice grew up to be the film actor Michael Caine. Families accommodating children were paid 8s 6d per week per child. Not everyone wanted to help, and some had to be compelled by law. Most did their bit willingly. When town met country there was a clash of cultures. Many Londoners had never been in rural areas before. Some locals questioned the sanitation habits of their guests. There was some misunderstanding, and some evacuees were luckier than others in their billets; some unfortunate ones were mistreated, had a terrible time, and had to be moved out. Everybody's story was different. The number of pupils in many schools doubled overnight, and in places local children were taught in the morning, evacuees in the afternoon. The newly arrived city children were taken on nature walks, encouraged to pick blackberries and take up other favourite country pursuits. As time went on, and everyone got used to each other in mutual adversity, there was tolerance on both sides.

How many came?

Officially three-and-a-half million people were moved to safe areas. They included 827,000 school-age children and 524,000 mothers with young children. As 1939 progressed the feared bombing did not materialise. As a result many evacuees went home. One estimate reckoned almost half of the 50,000 or more who arrived in Norfolk in September were back in London by January, 1940, particularly mothers with young children. The onset of the Blitz and the Battle of Britain later that year forced many back to the country. In June, 1940, following the fall of France and the expected seaborne invasion of southern England, more children were evacuated away from east and south coast ports. A further wave of bombing caused devastation during the summer of 1944. This time the attacks of the dreaded German V1 'doodleburgs' and V2 flying rockets caused havoc and terror, and led to a new wave of evacuations. In August that year an extra 3,000 children were sent to Norwich, so there were an estimated 20,000 evacuees in and around the city.

What was the legacy of evacuation?

Some, such as my own family, never returned to London. Their parents later joined them from the capital, and they settled in rural Norfolk. For all it was a formative experience, usually, though by no means always, for the better. Michael Caine was one who reckoned his life would have been different without enjoying the freedom and open spaces of the country at an early age. In November, 2003 he returned to North Runcton to unveil a plaque commemorating his association with the village school where he had passed his '11-plus' exam.

Select bibliography

Like all writers I owe a huge debt to a variety of primary and secondary sources. Below is a list of some of them.

The Anglo-Saxon Chronicles – anon
Ecclesiastical History of the English People – Bede
Beowulf – anon
The Peddars Way – Bruce Robinson
Folk Heroes of Britain – Charles Kightly
Folk Tales of the British Isles – Kevin Crossley-Holland
In Search of the Dark Ages – Michael Wood
Medieval Norwich – ed Carole Rawcliffe and Richard Wilson
Edward I, A Great and Terrible King – Marc Morris
Blood and Roses – Helen Castor
Cromwell, Our Chief of Men – Antonia Fraser
The King's War – C V Wedgwood
God's Englishman – Christopher Hill
Religion and the Decline of Magic – Keith Thomas
The Stripping of the Altars – Eamon Duffy
Amy Robsart of Wymondham – Sir Bartle Frere
The Book of Books – Melvyn Bragg
William Dowsing's Journal – ed Trevor Cooper
1666 Plague, War and Hellfire – Rebecca Rideal
Killers of the King – Charles Spencer
Britain and the World (1649-1815) – J R Jones
A History of Britain – Simon Schama
The Ascent of Money – Niall Ferguson
Norfolk Portraits, Norfolk Gallery and Norfolk in the Civil War – R W Ketton-Cremer
Faithful Handmaid: Fanny Burney at the Court of George III – Hester Davenport
Diary of a Country Parson – James Woodforde
The Slave Trade – Hugh Thomas
Thomas Clarkson, A Biography – Ellen Gibson Wilson
Norfolk Annals 1801-1850 – Charles Mackie
The Buildings of England – Nikolaus Pevsner and Bill Wilson
The Friends of Liberty – Albert Goodwin
The Making of the English Working Class – E P Thompson
More Than A Game – John Major
Ploughboy's Progress – Noel G Edwards

Also by Peter Sargent

A Moment in Time

50 stories that bring East Anglian history to life.

ISBN 9780995618718, published October 2017, price £12

In this series of short stories, encounter famous figures who made their mark on the eastern counties. Here is Oliver Cromwell raising an army, Queen Elizabeth I making a Royal Progress, while her sister Mary plays a game of thrones, highwayman Dick Turpin goes about his nefarious business and Norfolk squire and Britain's first Prime Minister, Robert Walpole, saves the country from financial ruin.

You'll also meet less familiar figures and veer off the beaten track. Here are tales of a Cambridgeshire Iron Age 'hill fort', Norfolk's raffish 19th Century bare knuckle boxers and the sailors who fought a huge, but barely remembered, 17th Century sea battle off the Suffolk coast.

"Peter Sargent has gathered together 50 stories from our past for a brilliant new book...A Moment in Time is a book that readers will want to dip into time and again to discover and rediscover the people and places that have helped shape our story." ***Let's Talk Magazine***